LEARN C SHARP

*Master Scalable Development with Modern Programming.
From Fundamentals to Practical Applications.*

Diego Rodrigues

LEARN C SHARP

Master Scalable Development with Modern Programming.
From Fundamentals to Practical Applications.

2025 Edition

Author: Diego Rodrigues

studiod21portoalegre@gmail.com

Published by StudioD21.

Important Note

The codes and scripts presented in this book are primarily intended to practically illustrate the concepts discussed throughout the chapters. They were developed to demonstrate educational applications in controlled environments and may therefore require adaptation to function correctly in different contexts. It is the reader's responsibility to validate the specific configurations of their development environment before practical implementation.

More than providing ready-made solutions, this book aims to foster a solid understanding of the topics covered, encouraging critical thinking and technical autonomy. The examples presented should be viewed as starting points for readers to develop their own original solutions tailored to the real demands of their careers or projects. True technical competence arises from the ability to internalize essential principles and apply them creatively, strategically, and transformatively.

We therefore encourage each reader to go beyond merely reproducing examples, using this content as a foundation to build scripts and code with their own identity—capable of making a significant impact on their professional journey. This is the essence of applied knowledge: learning deeply to innovate with purpose.

Thank you for your trust, and we wish you a productive and inspiring study journey.

CONTENTS

GREETINGS!

Hello, dear reader!

It is with great pleasure that I welcome you, who have decided to embark on this fascinating journey through the world of C#, one of the most powerful, versatile, and influential programming languages in today's technological landscape. Your choice to explore this subject demonstrates an admirable commitment to advancing your technical skills and a desire to master tools that transform ideas into practical and innovative solutions.

C# is much more than just a programming language. It is the backbone of modern applications ranging from robust corporate systems to immersive games developed with Unity. With C#, you don't just write code; you create, innovate, and push the boundaries of what is possible—whether in web application development, enterprise software, or devices connected to the Internet of Things.

In this book, you will find a clear and progressive path that takes you from the most essential fundamentals to practical and advanced applications in real and challenging projects. Our approach combines solid theory and dynamic practice, ensuring that you not only understand the fundamental concepts of C# but also gain the confidence needed to apply them in real-world situations.

It doesn't matter if you are a curious beginner, a programmer looking to expand your skills, or an experienced professional seeking to explore new horizons with C#. This book has been carefully designed to meet all experience levels. Each chapter has been crafted with attention to detail, providing engaging and impactful learning as you explore techniques that truly make a difference in the competitive market.

We live in an era where technology is at the center of everything, and mastering C# is an indispensable skill for any professional who wants to thrive in this environment. Whether developing enterprise systems, web applications, games, or smart devices, C# is a language that spans industries and connects people to creative and efficient solutions.

This book was created to be more than just a technical guide; it is an essential resource to fill editorial gaps, provide up-to-date knowledge, and strengthen the foundation of professionals in a market that never stops evolving. On every page, you will find stimulating challenges, clear explanations, and practical examples that make learning accessible, inspiring, and applicable.

Get ready to dive into a unique didactic experience, where you will learn to design, develop, and optimize applications with C# precisely and creatively. Together, we will explore the endless possibilities that C# offers and equip you with the tools needed to stand out in your career or personal projects.

So, are you ready to transform the way you create solutions and master one of the most impactful programming languages today? Let's get started!

ABOUT THE AUTHOR

Diego Rodrigues
Technical Author and Independent Researcher
ORCID: https://orcid.org/0009-0006-2178-634X
StudioD21 Smart Tech Content & Intell Systems
Email: studiod21portoalegre@gmail.com
LinkedIn: linkedin.com/in/diegoexpertai

International technical author (tech writer) focused on the structured production of applied knowledge. He is the founder of StudioD21 Smart Tech Content & Intell Systems, where he leads the creation of intelligent frameworks and the publication of didactic technical books supported by artificial intelligence, such as the Kali Linux Extreme series, SMARTBOOKS D21, among others.

Holder of 42 international certifications issued by institutions such as IBM, Google, Microsoft, AWS, Cisco, META, Ec-Council, Palo Alto, and Boston University, he works in the fields of Artificial Intelligence, Machine Learning, Data Science, Big Data, Blockchain, Connectivity Technologies, Ethical Hacking, and Threat Intelligence.

Since 2003, he has developed more than 200 technical projects for brands in Brazil, the USA, and Mexico. In 2024, he established himself as one of the leading technical book authors of the new generation, with over 180 titles published in six languages. His work is based on his proprietary TECHWRITE 2.3 applied technical writing protocol, focused on scalability, conceptual precision, and practical applicability in professional environments.

BOOK PRESENTATION

Welcome to LEARN C#: From Fundamentals to Practical Applications, a guide designed to transform the way you understand, apply, and master the C# programming language. This book is more than an introduction to the technology—it is a carefully planned journey to guide you from the basics to the advanced, offering a complete and applicable understanding of this powerful tool. Our goal is simple: to empower you to create practical, robust, and innovative solutions, regardless of your current level of experience.

C# is one of the most relevant languages of the modern era, widely used across various domains such as web development, game creation, and enterprise systems. With its clear syntax, versatility, and continuous support from Microsoft, C# has become a reliable choice for developers seeking efficiency and scalability. In this book, we show how this language can be used to turn ideas into real applications that add value, whether in the corporate world, entertainment, or connected devices.

If you are accessing this sample through Google Play Books or Amazon KDP, we want to emphasize the importance of mastering this guide. Each chapter has been meticulously designed to provide a complete, progressive, and practical learning experience. Throughout this journey, you will understand why C# is indispensable in today's landscape and how it can open doors to countless career opportunities.

Here is an overview of what you will find in each chapter:

Chapter 1. Introduction to C#: History and Applications

Discover how C# was born, evolved, and earned its place among the most important programming languages. Explore its applications in areas such as web development, games, and enterprise solutions, and understand why mastering this language is a strategic decision.

Chapter 2. Setting Up Your Development Environment

Learn how to set up an efficient environment for programming in C#. From installing Visual Studio to creating your first program, this chapter provides clear instructions so you can start your journey with confidence.

Chapter 3. Structure of a C# Program

Get to know the elements that make up a C# program, including namespaces, classes, and methods. Mastering this structure is essential to understanding how code is organized and executed.

Chapter 4. Data Types and Operators

Explore the various data types in C# and how they can be used to represent information. This chapter covers arithmetic, relational, and logical operators, preparing you to perform calculations and comparisons.

Chapter 5. Flow Control in C#

Learn to make decisions in code with conditional structures such as if, else, and switch. Also discover how for, while, and foreach loops help automate tasks.

Chapter 6. Functions and Methods

Understand how to create functions that make your code

modular and reusable. This chapter covers variable scope, parameter passing, and static and instance methods.

Chapter 7. Classes, Objects, and OOP
Object-oriented programming (OOP) is one of the pillars of C#. Here, you will learn about properties, methods, inheritance, and interfaces—essential elements for building well-structured programs.

Chapter 8. String Manipulation
Discover how to work with strings in C#, from simple operations like concatenation to advanced techniques such as manipulation with regular expressions.

Chapter 9. Collections and Data Structures
Dive into C# collections such as arrays, lists, and dictionaries. Learn how to choose the right structures to store and manage data efficiently.

Chapter 10. Exception Handling
Master the use of try, catch, and finally to handle errors in your code. This chapter teaches how to prevent failures and maintain the stability of your applications.

Chapter 11. Working with Files
Explore reading and writing files, stream manipulation, and data serialization. This chapter is essential for those who wish to work with data persistence.

Chapter 12. Asynchronous Programming with C#
Understand how to perform asynchronous operations with async and await. This chapter shows how C# makes it easier to

manage parallel tasks and improve application performance.

Chapter 13. LINQ: Language Integrated Query
Learn how to query collections and databases with LINQ. This chapter reveals how to simplify data manipulation with this powerful tool.

Chapter 14. Development with Windows Forms
Discover how to create graphical interfaces using Windows Forms. This chapter teaches everything from creating basic windows to handling events.

Chapter 15. Web Development with ASP.NET
Dive into web development with ASP.NET. Build modern, secure, and scalable applications by exploring concepts such as MVC and RESTful APIs.

Chapter 16. Database Integration
Learn how to connect your applications to databases, perform CRUD operations, and use Entity Framework to simplify working with data.

Chapter 17. Game Applications with Unity
Discover how C# is used to create games in Unity. This chapter presents the fundamentals of 2D and 3D game development.

Chapter 18. Security and Best Practices
Ensure the security of your applications with data validation techniques and protection against common vulnerabilities.

Chapter 19. Testing and Debugging Code

Learn to identify and correct errors in your code. This chapter covers testing and debugging tools to ensure the quality of your applications.

Chapter 20. Optimization and Performance

Improve your applications' performance with code optimization techniques and memory management.

Chapter 21. Working with External APIs

Discover how to integrate external services using REST and SOAP APIs. This chapter includes authentication and real-time data consumption.

Chapter 22. C# for IoT and Devices

Explore the use of C# on connected devices. This chapter covers everything from device communication to automation projects.

Chapter 23. Real Projects with C#

See how to apply everything you've learned in practical projects such as management systems and complete APIs.

Chapter 24. Future Trends of C#

Stay up to date with innovations in the language and .NET, as well as trends like artificial intelligence and IoT.

Chapter 25. Career Tips and Certifications

Prepare for the job market with guidance on interviews, certifications, and career planning.

This book has been structured to be an indispensable guide,

whether you are just starting out or already have experience with C#. On every page, you will find clear explanations, practical examples, and challenges that will solidify your learning. So, embark on this journey and discover how C# can transform the way you create and innovate. We are confident that this book will be a turning point in your professional journey.

CHAPTER 1. INTRODUCTION TO C#: HISTORY AND APPLICATIONS

The C# programming language emerged at a decisive moment in technology history. Created by Microsoft in the year 2000 as part of the .NET platform, its goal was to provide a modern, versatile, and robust language for software development. Inspired by languages such as C++, Java, and Object Pascal, C# combines the best elements of these technologies to meet the growing demands of the corporate software market, web applications, and game development.

In the early 2000s, Microsoft sought a language that not only unified object-oriented programming concepts but also ensured simplicity and efficiency. The idea was to create an alternative that could directly compete with Java, bringing innovations that would allow greater integration with the Windows ecosystem. Anders Hejlsberg, who had previously led the development of languages such as Turbo Pascal and Delphi, was responsible for designing C#. Since then, the language has gone through several updates, each introducing new features that have expanded its possibilities and maintained its relevance in the technology landscape.

C# was initially designed to be used in conjunction with the Common Language Runtime (CLR), which is part of the .NET Framework. This allowed developers to write code that could run on different platforms supported by Microsoft, while taking advantage of benefits such as automatic memory management and support for multiple languages. Over time, the evolution of .NET—including the introduction of .NET Core and, more recently, .NET 6 and .NET 7—has made C# a cross-platform tool, extending its applications to Linux, macOS, and even mobile devices.

The impact of C# goes far beyond the Microsoft ecosystem. It has become the primary choice for a wide range of projects due to its flexibility. The language is widely used in various industries, each leveraging its features to meet their specific needs.

In corporate systems development, C# is widely used to create robust and scalable applications. Organizations around the world rely on tools such as ASP.NET to build systems that support millions of users simultaneously, such as corporate portals, e-commerce platforms, and enterprise resource planning (ERP) systems.

In the field of web development, the language is one of the most popular thanks to its integration with ASP.NET Core. This technology enables the creation of modern, secure, and high-performance web applications. The modular structure of C# makes it easy to implement RESTful APIs, which are widely used in systems that require integration with other services.

The gaming industry has also embraced C#. Thanks to its integration with the Unity engine, the language has become a standard for 2D and 3D game development. Unity is used in projects ranging from indie games to big-budget productions, as well as virtual reality and augmented reality applications. With its clear syntax and wide range of available libraries, C# enables developers to create detailed and interactive virtual worlds.

Moreover, C# is becoming increasingly relevant in the Internet of Things (IoT). With the introduction of .NET IoT and compatibility with low-power devices such as the Raspberry Pi, developers can create solutions for home automation, environment monitoring, and connected devices. The combination of ease of use and performance makes the language ideal for systems where reliability and efficiency are critical.

Compared to other programming languages, C# offers a unique balance between performance and productivity. While languages such as C++ offer greater control over hardware, C# makes coding easier by abstracting complex details like memory management, allowing developers to focus on program logic. Compared to Java, C# offers a more modern syntax and advanced features such as LINQ (Language Integrated Query) and async/await for asynchronous programming, which are not available as efficiently on other platforms.

C#'s integration with .NET also sets it apart from languages such as Python and JavaScript. Although these are popular in areas such as data science and front-end development, respectively, C# shines in corporate systems and applications that require high performance. The continuous evolution of the language, with regular updates introducing new features and improvements, demonstrates Microsoft's commitment to keeping it competitive and relevant.

A practical application example of C# can be found in the development of an inventory management system for a retail company. With C#, it is possible to create a user-friendly graphical interface for employees to record product entries and exits, while a connected database, such as SQL Server, securely stores the information. Here is a code snippet that demonstrates how C# can be used to record a new entry in the database:

```
csharp
using System;
using System.Data.SqlClient;

class InventoryManagement
{
    static void Main()
```

```
    {
        string connectionString =
"Server=localhost;Database=InventoryDB;Trusted_Connection=
True;";
        string query = "INSERT INTO Products (ProductName,
Quantity, Price) VALUES (@name, @quantity, @price)";


        Console.Write("Enter product name: ");
        string name = Console.ReadLine();
        Console.Write("Enter quantity: ");
        int quantity = int.Parse(Console.ReadLine());
        Console.Write("Enter price: ");
        decimal price = decimal.Parse(Console.ReadLine());


        using (SqlConnection connection = new
SqlConnection(connectionString))
        {
            SqlCommand command = new SqlCommand(query,
connection);
            command.Parameters.AddWithValue("@name",
name);
            command.Parameters.AddWithValue("@quantity",
quantity);
            command.Parameters.AddWithValue("@price", price);


            connection.Open();
            int rowsAffected = command.ExecuteNonQuery();
```

```csharp
        Console.WriteLine($"{rowsAffected} row(s) inserted.");
    }
  }
}
```

The code above demonstrates the simplicity and clarity of C# when integrating an application with a relational database. It highlights features such as the use of parameterized variables, which help prevent SQL injection attacks, as well as encapsulating the connection logic within using blocks, ensuring proper resource closure.

Another strong point of C# is asynchronous programming, which is essential in modern applications that require high responsiveness. Using the async and await keywords, developers can implement non-blocking calls to external APIs or databases. See an example:

csharp

```csharp
using System;

using System.Net.Http;

using System.Threading.Tasks;


class AsyncExample

{

    static async Task Main()

    {

        string url = "https://api.example.com/data";
```

```csharp
using (HttpClient client = new HttpClient())
{
    Console.WriteLine("Fetching data...");
    string response = await client.GetStringAsync(url);
    Console.WriteLine("Data received:");
    Console.WriteLine(response);
}
}
```

The code above illustrates how C# enables network operations without blocking the main program flow. This approach is particularly useful in applications that require continuous interactivity, such as graphical interfaces or mobile apps.

Over the past two decades, C# has proven to be a language that adapts to market demands, from supporting legacy systems to the latest emerging technologies. Its role in corporate software development, games, and IoT, combined with its flexibility and ease of use, makes it an essential choice for developers seeking to build modern and scalable solutions.

CHAPTER 2. SETTING UP YOUR DEVELOPMENT ENVIRONMENT

Preparing an efficient development environment is the first step to unlocking the full potential of the C# language. Choosing and configuring the right tools ensures productivity and a smooth learning experience, allowing both beginner and experienced developers to get the most out of the language. This chapter covers the installation of Visual Studio—one of the most popular IDEs for working with C#—as well as exploring alternatives, running your first classic program, and adopting best configuration practices.

Installing and Configuring Visual Studio

Visual Studio is a powerful tool developed by Microsoft that provides an integrated environment for coding, debugging, and testing. Its popularity is due to its intuitive interface and robust support for C# project development. Before you begin, it is essential to download the latest version of Visual Studio from Microsoft's official website. Make sure to choose the edition that best fits your needs, such as the Community Edition, which is free and feature-rich.

After downloading the installer, follow these steps to configure your environment:

1. Open the Visual Studio installer.

2. On the workload selection screen, choose "Desktop Development with .NET." This option installs the necessary components to work with C#.

3. Include other features, such as "ASP.NET and web development," if you plan to build web applications in the future.

4. Complete the installation and launch Visual Studio.

When opening Visual Studio for the first time, you will be prompted to choose a theme for the interface and a set of keyboard shortcuts. It is recommended to select the "Visual Studio" layout to maximize compatibility with tutorials and examples. Additional customizations can be made later in the options menu.

Once Visual Studio is configured, create a new project by following these steps:

1. Click "Create a new project" on the start screen.

2. Select "Console Application (.NET Core)" and click "Next."

3. Enter a name for your project and choose the directory where it will be saved.

4. Confirm the settings and click "Create."

Visual Studio will automatically generate the project skeleton. From there, you are ready to start writing C# code.

First Run of a "Hello, World!" Program

The "Hello, World!" program is a traditional milestone when introducing any programming language. It demonstrates the basic concepts of syntax and console output. In the newly created project, the main class will already be set up, containing the Main method, which is the entry point of any C# program.

The default code will look like this:

csharp

```
using System;

namespace HelloWorldApp
{
    class Program
    {
        static void Main(string[] args)
        {
            Console.WriteLine("Hello, World!");
        }
    }
}
```

This code performs the following operations:

- The line using System; allows the use of the standard .NET library, which contains classes such as Console.

- The declaration namespace HelloWorldApp organizes the code in a defined scope, making reuse and maintenance easier.

- The class Program encapsulates the program logic.

- The Main method serves as the entry point, where program execution begins.

- The instruction Console.WriteLine("Hello, World!");

displays the message "Hello, World!" in the console.

To run the program, click "Start" or press the F5 key. The console will open and the message will be displayed. This basic interaction allows you to verify that the development environment was configured correctly.

Auxiliary Tools

In addition to Visual Studio, there are alternative and auxiliary tools that can enrich the C# development experience:

Visual Studio Code

Visual Studio Code, or VS Code, is a lightweight, cross-platform IDE that also supports C#. It is ideal for developers who prefer a minimalist approach or need a tool that works on different operating systems. To set up VS Code:

- Download the installer from the official VS Code website.

- Install the C# extension available in the integrated Marketplace.

- Make sure the .NET SDK is installed on your system.

- Create a Program.cs file in a new directory and use the following basic code:

```csharp
using System;

class Program
{
```

```
static void Main()
{

    Console.WriteLine("Hello, World!");

}
}
```

Open the integrated terminal and run the command dotnet run to compile and execute the program.

VS Code also supports debugging and IntelliSense, making it a versatile alternative to Visual Studio.

Command Line Tools

For developers who prefer to work with command lines, .NET CLI is an essential tool. It allows you to create, compile, and run projects without the need for a full IDE. After installing the .NET SDK, use the following basic commands:

To create a new console project:

javascript

```
dotnet new console -n HelloWorldApp
cd HelloWorldApp
```

To compile and run the project:

arduino

```
dotnet run
```

The .NET CLI is useful for quickly setting up projects, especially in server environments or for automation integrations.

Best Configuration Practices

Properly configuring the development environment is just the beginning. To maximize productivity and ensure code quality, some additional practices are recommended:

- **Project Organization**
  Structure your code logically to facilitate maintenance and scalability. Use folders to separate different components, such as models, controllers, and services.

- **Version Control**
  Use tools like Git to manage code changes. Set up a local repository or connect to platforms such as GitHub or Azure DevOps.

- **Useful Extensions**
  In Visual Studio, install extensions like Resharper to improve productivity, or in VS Code, include extensions like Prettier to keep your code consistently formatted.

- **Custom Shortcuts**
  Get familiar with keyboard shortcuts for frequent tasks, such as debugging, running, and navigating code. This saves time and increases efficiency.

- **Efficient Debugging**
  Use breakpoints in Visual Studio to inspect variables and identify errors during execution. The "Quick Watch" feature allows you to check the state of objects in real time.

- **Documentation**
  Add meaningful comments to your code, especially in complex methods. Visual Studio makes it easy to create XML documentation for classes and methods.

- **Test Configuration**
  Set up automated tests at the beginning of the project. This

helps identify regressions quickly and ensures that the code is working as expected.

Benefits of a Well-Configured Environment

A well-configured development environment not only improves productivity but also reduces errors and makes the learning process more enjoyable. It allows developers to focus their efforts on creating efficient solutions, rather than solving tool-related technical problems. Whether in Visual Studio, VS Code, or using the .NET CLI, the key to success is maintaining an organized, functional environment tailored to the needs of the project.

CHAPTER 3. STRUCTURE OF A C# PROGRAM

The structure of a C# program reflects the organization and clarity promoted by the language, composed of several components working together to form robust and readable applications. Understanding these components is essential to create efficient, reusable, and easy-to-maintain code. This module focuses on the fundamental elements of a C# program, including namespaces, classes, and methods, as well as addressing coding conventions and naming standards that foster best practices.

Basic Components of a C# Program

A C# program usually starts with the definition of namespaces, followed by the declaration of classes and methods. These elements form the structural foundation of any application and help organize code in a logical and hierarchical format.

Namespaces

Namespaces are used to organize code and prevent conflicts between class, method, or other entity names. They function as logical containers that group related elements, allowing different parts of an application to coexist without interference. By default, the System namespace is included in most C# programs, providing access to fundamental classes such as Console.

csharp

```
using System;
```

```
namespace MyApplication
{
    class Program
    {
        static void Main(string[] args)
        {
            Console.WriteLine("Welcome to MyApplication!");
        }
    }
}
```

This example uses the System namespace, which contains the Console class and allows the use of the WriteLine method. The MyApplication namespace organizes the code in a defined scope, ensuring that classes with the same name in other parts of the project do not cause conflicts.

Custom namespaces can be created to organize code according to the needs of the project. An example would be to divide functionalities into different namespaces such as Utilities, Models, and Services, making navigation in larger projects easier.

csharp

```
namespace MyApplication.Utilities
{
    public class MathHelper
    {
```

```csharp
    public static int Add(int a, int b)
    {
        return a + b;
    }
  }
}
```

The MyApplication.Utilities namespace encapsulates the MathHelper class, preventing interference with classes of the same name in other scopes.

Classes

Classes are the fundamental building blocks of object-oriented programming in C#. They encapsulate related data and behaviors, allowing them to be reused and maintained independently. Each class in C# can contain fields, properties, methods, and constructors.

csharp

```csharp
namespace MyApplication.Models
{
    public class Person
    {
        public string Name { get; set; }
        public int Age { get; set; }

        public void Greet()
        {
            Console.WriteLine($"Hello, my name is {Name} and I
```

```
am {Age} years old.");
    }
  }
}
```

The Person class defines two attributes, Name and Age, as well as a Greet method that displays a personalized message. By encapsulating these elements, the class offers a clear representation of a real-world object.

Classes can also include constructors, which are special methods used to initialize objects. A constructor can assign initial values to the class fields.

csharp

```
public Person(string name, int age)
{
    Name = name;
    Age = age;
}
```

Methods

Methods are code blocks that perform specific actions. They can receive parameters, return values, or simply perform operations. The Main method is the entry point of any C# application, where execution begins.

csharp

```
namespace MyApplication
{
    class Program
```

```
    {
        static void Main(string[] args)
        {
            int result = Add(5, 10);
            Console.WriteLine($"The result is {result}");
        }


        static int Add(int a, int b)
        {
            return a + b;
        }
    }
}
```

In the above model, the Add method receives two integer parameters and returns their sum. The call to Add occurs within the Main method, displaying the result in the console.

Methods can be overloaded, which means multiple versions of the same method can exist as long as they have different signatures.

csharp

```
public class Calculator
{
    public int Add(int a, int b)
    {
        return a + b;
```

```
}

public double Add(double a, double b)
{
    return a + b;
}
}
```

With this approach, the Add method can work with both integers and floating-point numbers, increasing its flexibility.

Coding Conventions

Coding conventions help maintain consistency and readability in code. Following established standards not only facilitates teamwork but also improves long-term maintenance.

Naming

Choosing clear and descriptive names is essential. In C#, different types of identifiers follow specific standards:

- Classes: class names should be written in PascalCase, with each word starting with a capital letter. Example: UserManager, PaymentProcessor.

- Methods: method names should also use PascalCase. Example: CalculateTotal, GetUserDetails.

- Properties: follow the same pattern as classes and methods. Example: OrderDate, CustomerName.

- Fields: private field names usually start with an underscore and use camelCase. Example: _userId, _isActive.

- Variables: local variables should use camelCase. Example: orderCount, userList.

Indentation and Spacing

C# adopts 4-space indentation to improve readability. Blank lines can be used to separate logically related code blocks, preventing clutter.

csharp

```csharp
public class Order
{
    private int _orderId;

    public int OrderId
    {
        get { return _orderId; }
        set { _orderId = value; }
    }
}
```

Comments

Comments should be used to explain code intent, especially in complex methods or logic. In C#, there are three main types of comments:

- Single-line comments: start with //.

- Multi-line comments: delimited by /* and */.

- XML documentation: used to generate automatic documentation, starting with ///.

csharp

```
/// <summary>
/// Calculates the total price of an order.
/// </summary>
/// <param name="quantity">The number of items.</param>
/// <param name="unitPrice">The price per item.</param>
/// <returns>The total price.</returns>
public double CalculateTotal(int quantity, double unitPrice)
{
    return quantity * unitPrice;
}
```

XML documentation provides detailed information that can be displayed in IDEs such as Visual Studio, making code easier to understand for other developers.

Recommended Practices in Development

In addition to naming and organizational conventions, adopting best practices ensures more efficient code that is less prone to errors:

- Avoid long methods: break down complex logic into smaller, more specific methods.

- Keep classes cohesive: each class should have a single responsibility, following the SRP (Single Responsibility Principle).

- Use properties instead of public fields: properties provide greater control over data access.

- Validate input: methods should check the parameters received to prevent unexpected behavior.

csharp

```csharp
public void SetAge(int age)
{
    if (age < 0 || age > 120)
    {
        throw new
ArgumentOutOfRangeException(nameof(age), "Age must be
between 0 and 120.");
    }


    Age = age;
}
```

Such precautions increase code robustness and reduce the occurrence of failures.

Integration of Components

A real program combines namespaces, classes, and methods to create complete functionalities. For example, when developing an order management system, different classes can represent entities such as customers, products, and orders.

csharp

```csharp
namespace MyApplication.Models
```

```
{
    public class Product
    {
        public string Name { get; set; }
        public decimal Price { get; set; }
    }

    public class Order
    {
        public int OrderId { get; set; }
        public List<Product> Products { get; set; }

        public decimal CalculateTotal()
        {
            return Products.Sum(product => product.Price);
        }
    }
}
```

In the example above, the Order class calculates the total based on product prices. By integrating these components, it is possible to build complex functionalities in a modular and scalable way.

Common Error Resolution

Error: Program failed to compile due to missing Main method.

Solution: Every C# program needs an entry point. Make sure the Main method is declared as static inside an accessible class, for example:

```
static void Main(string[] args) { }
```

Error: Name conflict between classes in different files.

Solution: Use distinct namespaces and organize each functional group in its own logical namespace, such as MyApplication.Services or MyApplication.Models, avoiding naming collisions.

Error: NullReferenceException when accessing object properties.

Solution: Check if instances were created before use. Employ null checks (if (obj != null)) or the null-coalescing operator (obj?.Property) to prevent runtime failures.

Best Practices

- Use custom namespaces to segment business logic and reduce circular dependencies.

- Apply method overloading only when there is a real need, avoiding ambiguity and maintaining clear signatures.

- Use XML comments consistently to allow automatic documentation generation and facilitate collaborative maintenance.

Strategic Summary

Understanding the structure of a C# program is mastering the foundation of modern code organization. The correct use of namespaces, classes, and methods ensures that the application grows in a modular, predictable, and easily scalable way. When the developer respects naming conventions and logical isolation, the result is an ecosystem of components that interact without conflict, reducing rework and increasing maintenance efficiency.

The technical application of these concepts drives the creation of robust business software. Each well-defined namespace and cohesive class contributes to safer code, with lower coupling and greater semantic clarity. This clear architecture underpins CI/CD practices, API integration, and future expansion, making mastery of C# structure an indispensable technical differentiator.

CHAPTER 4. DATA TYPES AND OPERATORS

The C# language offers a wide variety of data types and operators that allow you to represent and manipulate information effectively. Mastering these concepts is fundamental to creating solid and versatile applications, ensuring that data is processed correctly and that logical and arithmetic operations are performed precisely.

Data Types in C#

Data types in C# are categorized into two main groups: primitive and composite. Each type has specific characteristics that determine how values are stored and manipulated.

Primitive Types

Primitive types are the basic building blocks of any application. They are predefined by the language and include numbers, characters, and boolean values.

Numeric Types

Numeric types in C# can be integers or floating-point numbers. They are used to represent numeric values with different sizes and precision.

- byte: Represents 8-bit unsigned integers, ranging from 0 to 255.

- sbyte: Represents 8-bit signed integers, ranging from -128 to 127.

- short: Represents 16-bit signed integers, ranging from -32,768 to 32,767.

- ushort: Represents 16-bit unsigned integers, ranging from 0 to 65,535.

- int: Represents 32-bit signed integers, ranging from -2,147,483,648 to 2,147,483,647.

- uint: Represents 32-bit unsigned integers, ranging from 0 to 4,294,967,295.

- long: Represents 64-bit signed integers, ranging from -9,223,372,036,854,775,808 to 9,223,372,036,854,775,807.

- ulong: Represents 64-bit unsigned integers, ranging from 0 to 18,446,744,073,709,551,615.

Example of using integer numeric types:

csharp

```
int age = 30;
long population = 7800000000;
byte level = 255;


Console.WriteLine($"Age: {age}, Population: {population}, Level: {level}");
```

Floating-point types are used to represent values that include decimal places.

- float: Represents 32-bit floating-point numbers with

approximately 7 digits of precision.

- double: Represents 64-bit floating-point numbers with approximately 15–16 digits of precision.

- decimal: Represents 128-bit floating-point numbers, ideal for financial calculations due to greater precision.

Using floating-point numeric types:

csharp

```
float price = 19.99f;

double distance = 384400.5; // Distance from Earth to the Moon in kilometers.

decimal salary = 99999.99m;


Console.WriteLine($"Price: {price}, Distance: {distance}, Salary: {salary}");
```

Character Types

The char type is used to represent a single Unicode character.

csharp

```
char grade = 'A';
Console.WriteLine($"Grade: {grade}");
```

Boolean Types

The bool type is used to represent logical values: true or false.

csharp

```
bool isEligible = true;
```

```csharp
Console.WriteLine($"Is eligible: {isEligible}");
```

String Type

Although technically a composite type, string is widely used to manipulate text.

csharp

```csharp
string greeting = "Hello, World!";
Console.WriteLine(greeting);
```

Composite Types

Composite types allow you to create more complex structures, such as collections and objects.

Arrays

An array is a collection of elements of the same type.

csharp

```csharp
int[] numbers = { 1, 2, 3, 4, 5 };
Console.WriteLine($"First number: {numbers[0]}");
```

Lists

The List<T> class is a more flexible alternative to arrays.

csharp

```csharp
List<string> fruits = new List<string> { "Apple", "Banana", "Cherry" };
fruits.Add("Date");
```

```
Console.WriteLine($"Total fruits: {fruits.Count}");
```

Dictionaries

The Dictionary<TKey, TValue> class stores key-value pairs.

csharp

```
Dictionary<string, int> ages = new Dictionary<string, int>
{
    { "Alice", 30 },
    { "Bob", 25 }
};
Console.WriteLine($"Alice's age: {ages["Alice"]}");
```

Operators in C#

Operators are used to perform operations on variables and values. C# supports several types of operators, including arithmetic, relational, and logical.

Arithmetic Operators

Arithmetic operators perform basic mathematical calculations.

- +: Adds two values.

- -: Subtracts one value from another.

- *: Multiplies two values.

- /: Divides one value by another.

- %: Returns the remainder of a division.

csharp

```
int a = 10;
int b = 3;


Console.WriteLine($"Addition: {a + b}");
Console.WriteLine($"Subtraction: {a - b}");
Console.WriteLine($"Multiplication: {a * b}");
Console.WriteLine($"Division: {a / b}");
Console.WriteLine($"Modulus: {a % b}");
```

Relational Operators

Relational operators are used to compare values and return a boolean result.

- ==: Checks if two values are equal.

- !=: Checks if two values are different.

- >: Checks if the first value is greater than the second.

- <: Checks if the first value is less than the second.

- >=: Checks if the first value is greater than or equal to the second.

- <=: Checks if the first value is less than or equal to the second.

csharp

```
int x = 5;
```

```csharp
int y = 10;
```

```csharp
Console.WriteLine($"Equal: {x == y}");
Console.WriteLine($"Not equal: {x != y}");
Console.WriteLine($"Greater than: {x > y}");
Console.WriteLine($"Less than: {x < y}");
```

Logical Operators

Logical operators are used to combine boolean conditions.

- &&: Returns true if both conditions are true.

- ||: Returns true if at least one condition is true.

- !: Inverts the logical value.

csharp

```csharp
bool isAdult = true;
bool hasPermission = false;
```

```csharp
Console.WriteLine($"Can enter: {isAdult && hasPermission}");
Console.WriteLine($"Requires only one condition: {isAdult || hasPermission}");
Console.WriteLine($"Inverted: {!isAdult}");
```

Integration of Data Types and Operators

By combining data types and operators, you can create programs that perform complex calculations, evaluate conditions, and manage data.

csharp

```
int apples = 10;
int oranges = 15;
int totalFruits = apples + oranges;


bool moreApples = apples > oranges;


Console.WriteLine($"Total fruits: {totalFruits}");
Console.WriteLine($"More apples than oranges: {moreApples}");
```

Common Error Resolution

Error: Invalid conversion between numeric types.
Solution: Use explicit conversions when necessary. For example, when converting double to int, apply (int)value or use Convert.ToInt32(value) to avoid loss of precision and runtime exceptions.

Error: IndexOutOfRangeException when accessing array elements.
Solution: Always check the size of the collection before access using if (index < array.Length). This validation prevents access beyond array limits.

Error: Incorrect string comparison.
Solution: Use string.Equals(a, b, StringComparison.OrdinalIgnoreCase) for safe comparisons, avoiding failures caused by case sensitivity or regional settings.

Best Practices

- Prefer specific types (int, double, decimal) instead of generics (var) when clarity is more important than brevity.

- Use const and readonly for immutable values, ensuring integrity and preventing unwanted changes.

- Avoid mixing logical and arithmetic operations in the same expression; break them into steps to facilitate reading and debugging.

Strategic Summary

Mastering data types and operators in C# forms the foundation of every reliable application. Each numeric, boolean, or textual type has storage and performance characteristics that directly influence calculation precision and resource consumption. Understanding these details allows you to build more predictable systems, avoiding subtle runtime errors and reducing maintenance costs.

Operators, in turn, represent the bridge between logic and processing. When applied correctly, they allow intentions to be expressed clearly, efficiently, and safely. The combination of suitable types and well-used operators supports the creation of robust algorithms, ensuring that code maintains consistency and performance even in complex scenarios of integration and data analysis.

CHAPTER 5. FLOW CONTROL IN C#

Flow control in C# is essential for building programs that make decisions, iterate over data, and execute code blocks conditionally. It allows a program to behave dynamically, reacting to different inputs or states. This module is dedicated to the conditional structures if, else, and switch, as well as the repetition loops for, while, do-while, and the powerful foreach, along with iterators for efficient collection handling.

Conditional Structures

Conditional structures allow code to evaluate expressions and execute instruction blocks based on true or false results.

If and Else Structure

The if structure evaluates a boolean condition and executes the associated block if the condition is true. The use of else allows for an alternate block to be executed when the condition is not met.

csharp

```
int score = 85;


if (score >= 90)
{
    Console.WriteLine("Grade: A");
}
```

```csharp
else if (score >= 80)

{

    Console.WriteLine("Grade: B");

}

else

{

    Console.WriteLine("Grade: C");

}
```

This code evaluates the score and assigns a grade based on defined ranges. Conditional logic allows checking multiple conditions in sequence.

Switch Structure

The switch structure is ideal for evaluating a variable against different values and executing the corresponding block. It is more efficient than a series of if statements when conditions are based on specific values.

csharp

```csharp
string day = "Monday";


switch (day)

{

    case "Monday":

        Console.WriteLine("Start of the work week.");

        break;

    case "Friday":
```

```
    Console.WriteLine("End of the work week.");
    break;
case "Saturday":
case "Sunday":
    Console.WriteLine("Weekend!");
    break;
default:
    Console.WriteLine("Midweek day.");
    break;
}
```

The variable day is compared with several options, and the corresponding block is executed. The use of default ensures that an unexpected value is also handled.

Repetition Loops

Repetition loops allow code blocks to be executed multiple times based on conditions or data collections.

for Structure

The for structure is ideal when the number of iterations is known. It combines initialization, condition, and increment in a single line.

csharp

```
for (int i = 1; i <= 5; i++)
{
    Console.WriteLine($"Iteration: {i}");
}
```

The counter i is initialized at 1, and the loop continues while i is less than or equal to 5. After each iteration, the value of i is incremented.

while Structure

The while structure executes a code block while a boolean condition is true. It is used when the number of iterations is not known in advance.

csharp

```csharp
int count = 0;

while (count < 3)
{
    Console.WriteLine($"Count: {count}");
    count++;
}
```

The loop continues while count is less than 3. The increment within the block prevents infinite loops.

do-while Structure

The do-while structure ensures that the code block is executed at least once, since the condition is evaluated at the end.

csharp

```csharp
int number = 0;
```

```
do
{
    Console.WriteLine($"Number: {number}");
    number++;
} while (number < 2);
```

Even if the condition is false at the first check, the block is executed at least once.

Working with foreach and Iterators

foreach Structure

The foreach structure is used to iterate over collections such as arrays or lists in a simplified manner. It eliminates the need to manage indexes manually.

csharp

```
string[] fruits = { "Apple", "Banana", "Cherry" };

foreach (string fruit in fruits)
{
    Console.WriteLine(fruit);
}
```

Each element in the fruits collection is sequentially accessed and assigned to the variable fruit, allowing direct iteration over the elements.

Iterators

Iterators are used to create methods that return elements from a collection one at a time, using the yield keyword. They allow for custom loops for incremental access to data.

csharp

```csharp
IEnumerable<int> GenerateNumbers()
{
    for (int i = 1; i <= 5; i++)
    {
        yield return i;
    }
}


foreach (int number in GenerateNumbers())
{
    Console.WriteLine(number);
}
```

The GenerateNumbers method uses yield return to provide numbers from 1 to 5. The foreach structure consumes these values sequentially.

Combining Conditional Structures and Loops

By combining conditional structures and repetition loops, it is possible to create more complex and functional logic.

csharp

```csharp
int[] scores = { 95, 82, 74, 60 };

foreach (int score in scores)
{
    if (score >= 90)
    {
        Console.WriteLine($"Score: {score}, Grade: A");
    }
    else if (score >= 80)
    {
        Console.WriteLine($"Score: {score}, Grade: B");
    }
    else if (score >= 70)
    {
        Console.WriteLine($"Score: {score}, Grade: C");
    }
    else
    {
        Console.WriteLine($"Score: {score}, Grade: F");
    }
}
```

The scores collection is iterated, and each value is evaluated to determine a grade. This demonstrates how conditions and loops can be combined to process data efficiently.

Flow Control in Real Actions

Flow control structures are widely used in real scenarios, such as data validation, conditional task execution, and collection analysis.

User Input Validation:

csharp

```
int input;

do
{
    Console.WriteLine("Enter a number between 1 and 10:");
    input = int.Parse(Console.ReadLine());
} while (input < 1 || input > 10);

Console.WriteLine($"You entered: {input}");
```

The program prompts the user to enter a valid number, repeating until the input is within the specified range.

Collection Filters

csharp

```
int[] numbers = { 1, 2, 3, 4, 5, 6, 7, 8, 9, 10 };

foreach (int number in numbers)
{
```

```
if (number % 2 == 0)

{

    Console.WriteLine($"Even: {number}");

}

}
```

The example above analyzes a collection of numbers, displaying only the even ones. This illustrates how to apply conditional logic to filter data.

Common Error Resolution

Error: Infinite loop caused by incorrect condition.
Solution: Check if the control variable is updated within the loop. In while and do-while, increment or alter the value used in the condition to ensure correct termination.

Error: InvalidCastException when using switch with incompatible types.
Solution: Make sure that the type evaluated in the switch is compatible with the case values. Convert explicitly before comparison, if necessary.

Error: FormatException when reading numeric input from the console.
Solution: Replace int.Parse() with int.TryParse() to validate input before conversion, preventing unexpected interruptions during execution.

Best Practices

- Use foreach whenever possible to avoid manual index manipulation and reduce access errors in collections.

- Prefer switch in scenarios with multiple discrete

conditions for greater readability and efficiency.

- Avoid nesting too many if-else blocks; opt for short conditional expressions or extract logic to helper methods.

Strategic Summary

Flow control defines the logical behavior of an application. With the correct use of conditional structures and loops, it is possible to build predictable, efficient programs capable of reacting to different situations. Understanding execution order and condition evaluation is what allows static algorithms to become dynamic and interactive systems.

These structures also support modern development practices such as test automation and real-time decision pipelines. Knowing how to balance condition clarity with loop efficiency sets apart the average programmer from the engineer who masters end-to-end execution flow.

CHAPTER 6. FUNCTIONS AND METHODS

Functions and methods are fundamental in C# programming. They allow code blocks to be encapsulated, reused, and efficiently organized. Understanding these concepts enables you to build more modular, readable, and maintainable programs. In this chapter, we will explore the definition and use of functions, variable scope, parameter passing, and the distinction between static and instance methods.

Definition and Use of Functions

A function is a block of code that performs a specific task. In C#, functions are defined inside classes and are called methods. They can return values, receive parameters, or simply execute actions.

Structure of a Method

Methods have a basic structure that includes the return type, the method name, parameters (optional), and the code block.

csharp

```csharp
public int Add(int a, int b)
{
    return a + b;
}
```

In the example above, the method Add:

- Returns a value of type int.

- Receives two parameters of type int.

- Performs an addition and returns the result.

Calling a Method

To use a method, it must be invoked from an instance of the class (for instance methods) or directly by the class (for static methods).

csharp

```csharp
public class Calculator
{
    public int Add(int a, int b)
    {
        return a + b;
    }
}


// Calling the method
Calculator calculator = new Calculator();
int result = calculator.Add(5, 3);
Console.WriteLine($"The result is {result}");
```

The calculator object is created to access the Add method. The sum result is stored in result and displayed.

Variable Scope

Scope determines where a variable is accessible in code. In C#, there are three main types of scope: local, class, and global.

Local Scope

Local variables are defined inside methods and can only be accessed within those methods. They are created when the method is called and destroyed when the method ends.

csharp

```
public void DisplayMessage()
{
    string message = "Hello, World!";
    Console.WriteLine(message);
}
```

The variable message only exists inside the DisplayMessage method.

Class Scope

Class variables, also called fields, are defined directly in the class and can be accessed by all methods of the class.

csharp

```
public class Person
{
    private string name;
```

```csharp
public void SetName(string name)
{
    this.name = name;
}


public void Greet()
{
    Console.WriteLine($"Hello, {name}!");
}
}
```

The variable name is accessible in all methods of the Person class.

Global Scope

C# does not have global variables in the traditional sense. Instead, global data can be simulated using static variables in classes.

csharp

```
public static class Globals
{
    public static string AppName = "My Application";
}
```

The variable AppName can be accessed globally anywhere in the program.

Parameter Passing

Methods can receive data via parameters. In C#, parameters can be passed by value, by reference, or as optional values.

Pass by Value

By default, parameters are passed by value, meaning a copy of the value is used inside the method.

csharp

```csharp
public void Increment(int number)
{
    number++;
    Console.WriteLine($"Inside method: {number}");
}


int value = 5;
Increment(value);
Console.WriteLine($"Outside method: {value}");
```

The change to the variable number does not affect the value of value outside the method.

Pass by Reference

Using the ref keyword, parameters are passed by reference,

allowing the method to change the original value.

csharp

```csharp
public void Increment(ref int number)
{
    number++;
    Console.WriteLine($"Inside method: {number}");
}


int value = 5;
Increment(ref value);
Console.WriteLine($"Outside method: {value}");
```

With ref, the change made in the method is reflected in the original variable.

Optional Parameters

Methods can define default values for parameters, making them optional.

csharp

```csharp
public void Greet(string name = "Guest")
{
    Console.WriteLine($"Hello, {name}!");
}


Greet(); // Uses the default value "Guest"
Greet("Alice"); // Overrides the default value
```

Static and Instance Methods

Static Methods

Static methods belong to the class and not to a specific instance. They can be called directly by the class name.

csharp

```csharp
public static class MathUtils
{
    public static int Multiply(int a, int b)
    {
        return a * b;
    }
}


int product = MathUtils.Multiply(4, 5);
Console.WriteLine($"Product: {product}");
```

Static methods are ideal for operations that do not depend on the internal state of the class.

Instance Methods

Instance methods depend on a specific instance of the class to be called. They have access to the fields and properties of the class.

csharp

```csharp
public class Rectangle
{
    public int Width { get; set; }
    public int Height { get; set; }

    public int CalculateArea()
    {
        return Width * Height;
    }
}

Rectangle rect = new Rectangle { Width = 10, Height = 5 };
int area = rect.CalculateArea();
Console.WriteLine($"Area: {area}");
```

The area of the rectangle is calculated based on the Width and Height values associated with the rect instance.

Method Overloading

Methods can be overloaded to handle different sets of parameters, as long as the signatures are unique.

csharp

```csharp
public class Printer
```

```csharp
{
    public void Print(string message)
    {
        Console.WriteLine(message);
    }

    public void Print(int number)
    {
        Console.WriteLine($"Number: {number}");
    }
}


Printer printer = new Printer();
printer.Print("Hello");
printer.Print(123);
```

Overloading allows the same method to process different data types.

Asynchronous Methods

Asynchronous methods perform long-running operations without blocking the main program flow. They are declared with the async keyword and often use await.

csharp

```csharp
public async Task<string> FetchDataAsync()
{
```

```
    await Task.Delay(2000); // Simulates a delay
    return "Data fetched successfully";
}


public async Task DisplayDataAsync()
{
    string data = await FetchDataAsync();
    Console.WriteLine(data);
}


await DisplayDataAsync();
```

Asynchronous methods are essential for improving the responsiveness of applications that perform I/O operations or network queries.

Common Error Resolution

Error: Incorrect call of a static method from an instance.
Solution: Static methods must be called directly by the class name, not by an object. For example, use MathUtils.Multiply(2, 3) instead of creating an instance of MathUtils.

Error: NullReferenceException when accessing uninitialized instance variables.
Solution: Ensure that the object is instantiated before calling the method. Example: Person p = new Person(); p.SetName("Ana"); avoids the error.

Error: Unexpected modification of parameters inside methods.
Solution: Use pass by value to protect external variables. Use ref only when changing the original value is intentional and

necessary.

Best Practices

- Use static methods only when the logic does not depend on the internal state of the class.

- Define descriptive method names, preferably with action verbs in the infinitive form, such as CalculateTotal or SendMessage.

- Apply overloading judiciously, ensuring that each version of the method has a distinct purpose and signature.

Strategic Summary

Functions and methods form the logical core of any C# application. Correct definition of scope and parameter passing determines code predictability and safety. Understanding the difference between instance and static methods is essential for modeling reusable behaviors and reducing dependencies. Conscious use of optional parameters and overloading increases flexibility without compromising clarity.

The adoption of asynchronous methods reflects maturity in modern development, allowing intensive tasks to occur without blocking the main flow. Applying this approach improves responsiveness and prepares the system for distributed environments. Implementing these techniques is a decisive step toward creating scalable, clean solutions aligned with C# engineering best practices.

CHAPTER 7. CLASSES, OBJECTS, AND OBJECT-ORIENTED PROGRAMMING

Object-oriented programming (OOP) is a paradigm that organizes software around objects, which are representations of real-world or abstract entities. In C#, OOP is central to building modular, scalable, and maintainable applications. This chapter details the fundamentals of OOP, including classes and objects, properties, methods, and encapsulation, as well as advanced concepts such as inheritance, polymorphism, and interfaces.

Fundamentals of Object-Oriented Programming

OOP is based on four main pillars: abstraction, encapsulation, inheritance, and polymorphism. These concepts make it easier to model complex systems, allowing parts of the code to be efficiently reused and maintained.

- **Abstraction** simplifies the representation of entities by focusing on relevant characteristics and ignoring unnecessary details.

- **Encapsulation** protects the internal state of objects, restricting direct access to their members.

- **Inheritance** allows classes to share behaviors and properties, promoting code reuse.

- **Polymorphism** enables objects to assume different forms, providing flexibility to the code.

Classes and Objects

Classes are structures that define the properties and behaviors of an object. An object is an instance of a class containing specific values for its properties.

Defining a Class

A class is created with the class keyword. Its members include fields, properties, and methods.

csharp

```csharp
public class Person
{
    public string Name { get; set; }
    public int Age { get; set; }


    public void Greet()
    {
        Console.WriteLine($"Hello, my name is {Name} and I am {Age} years old.");
    }
}
```

The Person class has two properties (Name and Age) and a method (Greet) that prints a personalized greeting.

Creating Objects

Objects are created from classes using the new keyword.

csharp

```csharp
Person person = new Person();
person.Name = "Alice";
person.Age = 30;
person.Greet();
```

The person object is instantiated with specific values for Name and Age. The Greet method uses these values to display a message.

Properties, Methods, and Encapsulation

Properties and methods are essential elements of a class. Encapsulation ensures that access to class members is controlled, promoting security and integrity.

Properties

Properties provide a safe way to expose the fields of a class. In C#, they are usually defined with get and set accessors.

csharp

```
public class Product
{
    private decimal price;

    public decimal Price
    {
        get { return price; }
        set
```

```
    {
        if (value < 0)
        {
            throw new ArgumentException("Price cannot be
negative.");
        }
        price = value;
    }
  }
}
```

The Price property controls access to the private field price, ensuring that invalid values are not assigned.

Methods

Methods encapsulate logic that can be executed by objects of the class.

csharp

```csharp
public class Calculator
{
    public int Add(int a, int b)
    {
        return a + b;
    }
}
```

The Add method accepts two parameters and returns their sum.

Encapsulation

Encapsulation is implemented using access modifiers such as public, private, and protected.

- public: Allows access from anywhere.

- private: Restricts access to members of the same class.

- protected: Allows access to derived classes.

csharp
```csharp
public class BankAccount
{
    private decimal balance;

    public void Deposit(decimal amount)
    {
        if (amount <= 0)
        {
            throw new ArgumentException("Amount must be positive.");
        }
        balance += amount;
    }
```

```csharp
    public decimal GetBalance()
    {
        return balance;
    }
}
```

The `BankAccount` class encapsulates the `balance` variable, allowing it to be manipulated only through specific methods.

Inheritance

Inheritance allows a class to inherit members from another, avoiding code duplication.

csharp

```csharp
public class Animal
{
    public string Name { get; set; }

    public void Eat()
    {
        Console.WriteLine($"{Name} is eating.");
    }
}

public class Dog : Animal
```

```
{

    public void Bark()

    {

        Console.WriteLine($"{Name} is barking.");

    }

}
```

The Dog class inherits the Name property and the Eat method from the Animal class, and also defines its own Bark method.

Method Overriding

A derived class can override a method from the base class using the override keyword.

csharp

```
public class Cat : Animal

{

    public override void Eat()

    {

        Console.WriteLine($"{Name} is eating cat food.");

    }

}
```

The Eat method in the Cat class redefines the behavior of the base class method.

Polymorphism

Polymorphism allows objects of derived classes to be treated as objects of the base class.

csharp

```
Animal animal = new Dog();

animal.Name = "Buddy";

animal.Eat();

// animal.Bark(); // Not accessible, since the reference type is
Animal.
```

The animal object can access members of the Animal base class, but not members specific to the Dog class.

Polymorphism with Virtual Methods

Methods defined as virtual in the base class can be overridden in derived classes, allowing different behaviors.

csharp

```
public class Bird : Animal

{

    public override void Eat()

    {

        Console.WriteLine($"{Name} is eating seeds.");

    }

}
```

When the Eat method is called on a Bird object, the overridden behavior is executed.

Interfaces

Interfaces define a contract that classes must implement. They provide flexibility in development, allowing different classes to share common behaviors.

csharp

```csharp
public interface IFlyable
{
    void Fly();
}


public class Airplane : IFlyable
{
    public void Fly()
    {
        Console.WriteLine("Airplane is flying.");
    }
}


public class Bird : IFlyable
{
    public void Fly()
    {
        Console.WriteLine("Bird is flying.");
    }
}
```

The IFlyable interface is implemented by the Airplane and Bird classes, ensuring that both have the Fly method.

Using Interfaces

Interfaces allow you to create generic methods that accept any object implementing the interface.

csharp

```csharp
public void MakeFly(IFlyable flyable)
{
    flyable.Fly();
}


MakeFly(new Airplane());
MakeFly(new Bird());
```

The MakeFly method works with any object that implements IFlyable.

Combining Concepts

By combining classes, inheritance, polymorphism, and interfaces, you can create complex and flexible systems.

csharp

```csharp
public abstract class Shape
{
    public abstract double GetArea();
```

```
}


public class Circle : Shape
{
    public double Radius { get; set; }

    public override double GetArea()
    {
        return Math.PI * Radius * Radius;
    }
}


public class Rectangle : Shape
{
    public double Width { get; set; }
    public double Height { get; set; }

    public override double GetArea()
    {
        return Width * Height;
    }
}
```

The Shape class is abstract and defines the contract for calculating area. The Circle and Rectangle classes implement the specific behavior according to their shapes.

csharp

```
List<Shape> shapes = new List<Shape>
{
    new Circle { Radius = 5 },
    new Rectangle { Width = 10, Height = 4 }
};


foreach (Shape shape in shapes)
{
    Console.WriteLine($"Area: {shape.GetArea()}");
}
```

The shapes list contains objects of different types, but all are handled uniformly thanks to polymorphism.

Common Error Resolution

Error: Attempt to access a private member outside the class.
Solution: Use public properties with get and set or public controller methods to expose data securely.

Error: Failure to override a method without the correct keyword.
Solution: Use override on inherited methods and virtual in the base class to ensure valid polymorphic behavior.

Error: Partial interface implementation.
Solution: Ensure that all signatures defined in the interface are implemented in the class. The compiler does not allow omissions.

Best Practices

- Use encapsulation to protect internal state and avoid direct access to sensitive fields.

- Prefer inheritance only when there is a clear hierarchical relationship; otherwise, opt for composition.

- Use interfaces to define contracts and promote flexibility in extensible systems.

Strategic Summary

Object-oriented programming organizes code around concrete and abstract entities, creating coherent and reusable structures. Each class defines specific behaviors and interacts with others through contracts and inheritance, forming a solid foundation for any application. Encapsulation ensures security, while inheritance and polymorphism reduce duplication and enhance adaptability.

Applying these concepts technically transforms isolated instructions into consistent, evolving systems. By technically applying classes, objects, and interfaces, the developer gains control over structure, extensibility, and maintenance, achieving a balance between clarity and performance.

CHAPTER 8. STRING MANIPULATION

String manipulation is an essential skill in C#, as text is one of the most common data types in any application. Strings represent sequences of characters and can be used to store information such as names, addresses, and messages. In this chapter, we will cover basic and advanced string operations, formatting, searching and text manipulation, and introduce the use of regular expressions for working with complex patterns.

Basic String Operations

Strings in C# are immutable objects of the System.String class. This means that after they are created, they cannot be changed. Any modification creates a new string.

Creating Strings

A string can be created in various ways, from simple literals to concatenations.

csharp

```
string greeting = "Hello, World!";
string name = "Alice";
string combined = greeting + " My name is " + name + ".";
Console.WriteLine(combined);
```

Concatenation joins multiple strings into one. In this example, combined contains the greeting followed by the name.

Common Methods

The String class offers several methods for manipulating text.

- Length: Returns the number of characters.

- ToUpper and ToLower: Convert to uppercase and lowercase.

- Trim: Removes whitespace from the beginning and end.

- Substring: Returns a part of the string.

csharp

```
string message = " Hello, C# ";
Console.WriteLine(message.Trim());
Console.WriteLine(message.ToUpper());
Console.WriteLine(message.Substring(2, 5));
```

String Interpolation

Interpolation lets you create strings by combining literal text with variables in a readable way.

csharp

```
int age = 30;
string interpolated = $"I am {age} years old.";
Console.WriteLine(interpolated);
```

Interpolation uses $ before the string and includes variables inside curly braces {}.

Advanced String Operations

Splitting and Joining

Splitting divides a string into parts based on a delimiter, while joining combines elements of an array into a single string.

csharp

```csharp
string csv = "apple,banana,cherry";
string[] fruits = csv.Split(',');
foreach (string fruit in fruits)
{
    Console.WriteLine(fruit);
}


string joined = string.Join(", ", fruits);
Console.WriteLine(joined);
```

The Split method creates an array with the parts separated by commas, while Join combines them back.

Replacement

Replacement swaps parts of a string for other values.

csharp

```csharp
string sentence = "I love programming.";
string updated = sentence.Replace("love", "enjoy");
Console.WriteLine(updated);
```

The Replace method replaces all occurrences of a substring with the new string.

Comparison

C# offers methods for comparing strings, such as Equals, which checks if two strings are equal.

csharp

```csharp
string a = "hello";
string b = "HELLO";

bool caseSensitive = a.Equals(b);
bool caseInsensitive = a.Equals(b,
StringComparison.OrdinalIgnoreCase);

Console.WriteLine(caseSensitive); // False
Console.WriteLine(caseInsensitive); // True
```

The StringComparison.OrdinalIgnoreCase parameter allows for case-insensitive comparison.

String Formatting

Formatting enables you to create structured strings to display data in a readable way.

Format Method

The Format method inserts values into numbered placeholders.

csharp

```
string formatted = string.Format("My name is {0} and I am {1} years old.", "Alice", 30);
Console.WriteLine(formatted);
```

Placeholders {0} and {1} are replaced with the provided values.

Custom Strings

Custom formatting is used to display numbers and dates in specific ways.

csharp

```
decimal price = 19.99m;
DateTime today = DateTime.Now;


Console.WriteLine(price.ToString("C")); // Currency format
Console.WriteLine(today.ToString("yyyy-MM-dd")); // Date format
```

The formats C and yyyy-MM-dd display values in specific representations.

Searching and Manipulating Text

Finding Substrings

Substring location identifies where specific parts of a string appear.

csharp

```
string phrase = "The quick brown fox jumps over the lazy dog.";
int index = phrase.IndexOf("fox");
Console.WriteLine($"'fox' found at index: {index}");
```

The IndexOf method returns the starting position of the substring. If not found, it returns -1.

Checking Start and End

The StartsWith and EndsWith methods check if a string begins or ends with a specific substring.

csharp

```
string url = "https://example.com";

bool isSecure = url.StartsWith("https");
bool hasExtension = url.EndsWith(".com");

Console.WriteLine($"Secure: {isSecure}, Has .com: {hasExtension}");
```

Removing Parts

Parts of a string can be removed with the Remove method.

csharp

```
string text = "Hello, World!";

string shortened = text.Remove(5); // Removes from index 5
onward

Console.WriteLine(shortened);
```

The Remove method returns a new string without the specified characters.

Introduction to Regular Expressions

Regular expressions are powerful tools for searching, validating, and manipulating text based on patterns. In C#, they are implemented by the Regex class.

Format Validation

A regular expression can validate whether text follows a specific format, such as an email address.

csharp

```
using System.Text.RegularExpressions;


string email = "user@example.com";

string pattern = @"^[^@\s]+@[^@\s]+\.[^@\s]+$";
```

```csharp
bool isValid = Regex.IsMatch(email, pattern);
Console.WriteLine($"Valid email: {isValid}");
```

The pattern `^[^@\s]+@[^@\s]+\.[^@\s]+$` checks for a basic email format.

Pattern-Based Replacement

Replacement with regular expressions changes parts of text that match a pattern.

csharp

```csharp
string input = "Phone: 123-456-7890";
string sanitized = Regex.Replace(input, @"\d", "*");
Console.WriteLine(sanitized);
```

The pattern `\d` matches numeric digits, replacing them with asterisks.

Data Extraction

Extraction allows you to capture specific parts of text.

csharp

```csharp
string data = "Order ID: 12345, Total: $678.90";
string orderPattern = @"Order ID: (\d+)";
string totalPattern = @"Total: \$(\d+\.\d{2})";


Match orderMatch = Regex.Match(data, orderPattern);
```

```csharp
Match totalMatch = Regex.Match(data, totalPattern);

if (orderMatch.Success && totalMatch.Success)
{
    Console.WriteLine($"Order ID: {orderMatch.Groups[1].Value}");
    Console.WriteLine($"Total: {totalMatch.Groups[1].Value}");
}
```

The Match method searches for patterns and returns captured groups, allowing direct access to relevant parts.

Combining Techniques

Advanced string manipulation often combines multiple techniques to solve practical problems.

csharp

```csharp
string log = "ERROR: Disk full\nINFO: Backup completed \nWARNING: Low memory";

string[] lines = log.Split('\n');


foreach (string line in lines)
{
    if (line.StartsWith("ERROR"))
    {
        Console.WriteLine($"Error log: {line}");
    }
```

```
}
```

Splitting text into lines, combined with start checks, processes only the relevant entries.

Common Error Resolution

Error: Index out of range when using Substring or Remove.
Solution: Check that the index is less than the string length before the operation.

Error: Incorrect comparison due to case sensitivity.
Solution: Use StringComparison.OrdinalIgnoreCase in comparison methods.

Error: Invalid regular expression pattern.
Solution: Test the pattern before use and wrap the Regex.Match call in exception handling.

Best Practices

- Use string interpolation instead of concatenation for better readability.

- Employ StringBuilder in repetitive text modification operations.

- Keep regular expression patterns organized as reusable constants.

Strategic Summary

String manipulation in C# is a versatile skill that enables you to work with text efficiently and powerfully. Understanding both basic and advanced operations, combined with the use of regular expressions, prepares developers to handle real-world challenges in any application. With these tools, you can process, validate, and transform textual data reliably and effectively.

CHAPTER 9. COLLECTIONS AND DATA STRUCTURES

Collections and data structures are fundamental components for storing, organizing, and manipulating information in C# programs. They allow efficient data management—whether for batch processing, searching, or maintaining relationships between values. In this chapter, we cover arrays, lists, dictionaries, and other types of collections, exploring common operations and best practices to maximize code performance and readability.

Arrays

Arrays are static data structures that store elements of the same type. They are ideal for scenarios where the number of elements is known and fixed.

Declaration and Initialization

An array is declared by specifying the element type followed by []. It can be initialized with predefined values or allocated dynamically.

csharp

```
int[] numbers = { 1, 2, 3, 4, 5 };

string[] names = new string[3];

names[0] = "Alice";

names[1] = "Bob";

names[2] = "Charlie";
```

The numbers array contains five integers, while names is allocated with three positions, later filled.

Accessing Elements

Array elements are accessed by index, which starts at zero.

csharp

```csharp
Console.WriteLine(numbers[2]); // Prints the third element
numbers[4] = 10; // Updates the fifth element
```

The index must be within the array bounds; otherwise, an exception will be thrown.

Iterating Over Arrays

Arrays can be traversed with loop structures such as for or foreach.

csharp

```csharp
foreach (int number in numbers)
{
    Console.WriteLine(number);
}
```

Using foreach eliminates the need to manage indexes manually.

Lists

Lists are dynamic collections that can store elements more

flexibly than arrays. The List<T> class is widely used for its ease of use and versatility.

Declaration and Adding Elements

A list is declared by specifying the element type between < >. Elements can be added at any time using the Add method.

csharp

```
List<string> fruits = new List<string>();

fruits.Add("Apple");

fruits.Add("Banana");

fruits.Add("Cherry");
```

The fruits list grows dynamically as new elements are added.

Access and Modification

List elements can be accessed by index and modified directly.

csharp

```
Console.WriteLine(fruits[1]); // Prints "Banana"

fruits[2] = "Blueberry"; // Replaces "Cherry" with "Blueberry"
```

Removing Elements

The Remove and RemoveAt methods are used to delete elements.

csharp

```
fruits.Remove("Banana"); // Removes "Banana" by value

fruits.RemoveAt(0); // Removes the first element
```

Common Operations

The List<T> class offers methods such as Sort to sort elements and Contains to check if a value is present.

csharp

```
fruits.Sort();
bool hasApple = fruits.Contains("Apple");
```

Dictionaries

Dictionaries store key-value pairs, allowing efficient access to values via their keys. The Dictionary<TKey, TValue> class is the standard implementation in C#.

Declaration and Adding Pairs

A dictionary is declared by specifying the key and value types.

csharp

```
Dictionary<string, int> ages = new Dictionary<string, int>();
ages.Add("Alice", 30);
ages.Add("Bob", 25);
```

Keys must be unique, while values can be duplicated.

Accessing Values

Values are accessed via their associated keys.

csharp

```csharp
Console.WriteLine(ages["Alice"]); // Prints 30
```

If the key does not exist, an exception is thrown. The TryGetValue method can be used to avoid errors.

csharp

```csharp
if (ages.TryGetValue("Charlie", out int age))
{
    Console.WriteLine(age);
}
else
{
    Console.WriteLine("Key not found.");
}
```

Removing Pairs

The Remove method deletes a key-value pair from the dictionary.

charp

```csharp
ages.Remove("Bob");
```

Other Collection Types

HashSet

HashSet<T> is a collection that stores unique elements, ideal for avoiding duplicates.

```csharp
HashSet<int> uniqueNumbers = new HashSet<int> { 1, 2, 3, 1 };
Console.WriteLine(uniqueNumbers.Count); // Prints 3
```

Queue

The Queue<T> class implements a queue (FIFO - First In, First Out).

```csharp
Queue<string> tasks = new Queue<string>();
tasks.Enqueue("Task 1");
tasks.Enqueue("Task 2");
Console.WriteLine(tasks.Dequeue()); // Removes and prints "Task 1"
```

Stack

The Stack<T> class implements a stack (LIFO - Last In, First Out).

```csharp
Stack<string> history = new Stack<string>();
history.Push("Page 1");
history.Push("Page 2");
Console.WriteLine(history.Pop()); // Removes and prints "Page 2"
```

Best Practices for Using Collections

Choosing the Right Structure:

Choose the appropriate collection depending on the scenario:

- Use arrays when the size is fixed.

- Use lists for dynamic manipulation.

- Use dictionaries for key-value relationships.

- Use HashSet to ensure uniqueness.

- Use queues or stacks for managing the order of elements.

Avoid Modifications During Iteration

Modifying collections while iterating over them can cause exceptions. To avoid this, use a copy of the collection or methods that do not affect the original state.

csharp

```csharp
foreach (string fruit in fruits.ToList())
{
    if (fruit.StartsWith("A"))
    {
        fruits.Remove(fruit);
    }
}
```

Use LINQ Methods

LINQ (Language Integrated Query) simplifies operations on collections, such as filtering, sorting, and projections.

csharp

```csharp
var filteredFruits = fruits.Where(f => f.Contains("e")).ToList();
```

```
filteredFruits.ForEach(Console.WriteLine);
```

Avoid Memory Overload

Large collections can consume a lot of memory. Use methods like TrimExcess to optimize memory usage.

csharp

```
fruits.TrimExcess();
```

Common Error Resolution

Error: Index out of bounds when accessing arrays or lists.
Solution: Check the collection size with Length or Count before accessing.

Error: Removing elements during iteration.
Solution: Use a copy with ToList() or store items to remove in a temporary list before deletion.

Error: Duplicate key in dictionary.
Solution: Validate with ContainsKey before using Add or use TryAdd for safe insertions.

Best Practices

- Choose the collection based on the nature of the data and the frequency of access.

- Prefer var when declaring collections with explicit initialization for greater clarity and less type repetition.

- Use TrimExcess and Clear to control memory usage in dynamic collections.

Strategic Summary

Collections structure data storage and manipulation in C#. Arrays provide predictable performance in fixed scenarios, while lists and dictionaries offer flexibility and direct access to information. Proper use of each structure reduces resource consumption and simplifies code maintenance. Combined with LINQ, they expand query and filtering capabilities, allowing you to solve complex tasks with short and efficient expressions.

CHAPTER 10. EXCEPTION HANDLING

Exception handling is an essential component in developing robust software. In C#, it allows errors to be detected and handled in a controlled manner, preventing failures that could interrupt program execution. In this chapter, we explore the error control structures try, catch, and finally, creating custom exceptions, and best error-handling practices, ensuring that applications are resilient and reliable.

Error Control Structures

The most common approach to handling errors in C# uses the try, catch, and finally structures. These constructs allow you to capture exceptions, execute recovery actions, and ensure resources are released properly.

try Block

The try block contains code that may generate an exception. If an exception occurs, control is transferred to the corresponding catch block.

csharp

```
try
{
    int[] numbers = { 1, 2, 3 };
```

```
    Console.WriteLine(numbers[5]); // Generates an exception
}
catch (IndexOutOfRangeException ex)
{
    Console.WriteLine($"Error: {ex.Message}");
}
```

In this example, attempting to access an invalid index in an array generates an IndexOutOfRangeException, which is captured and handled in the catch block.

catch Block

The catch block captures the generated exception and contains the code to handle the error. You can specify the type of exception to be caught.

csharp

```
try
{
    int result = 10 / 0;
}
catch (DivideByZeroException ex)
{
    Console.WriteLine("Cannot divide by zero.");
}
```

The DivideByZeroException is captured and handled with a

specific message.

finally Block

The finally block contains code that must be executed whether or not an exception is thrown. It is useful for releasing resources such as database connections or files.

csharp

```
try
{
    using (StreamReader reader = new StreamReader("file.txt"))
    {
        string content = reader.ReadToEnd();
        Console.WriteLine(content);
    }
}
catch (FileNotFoundException ex)
{
    Console.WriteLine("File not found.");
}
finally
{
    Console.WriteLine("Execution completed.");
}
```

The finally block ensures that the message "Execution completed." is displayed, even if an exception occurs.

Creating Custom Exceptions

Although .NET provides several predefined exception classes, you can create custom exceptions to represent errors specific to your domain or application.

Defining a Custom Exception

A custom exception class should inherit from Exception and usually include additional constructors to provide detailed information.

csharp

```
public class InvalidAgeException : Exception
{
    public InvalidAgeException() : base("Age is not valid.") { }

    public InvalidAgeException(string message) : base(message) { }

    public InvalidAgeException(string message, Exception innerException)
        : base(message, innerException) { }
}
```

The InvalidAgeException represents an error related to invalid ages.

Throwing Custom Exceptions

Custom exceptions can be thrown using the throw keyword.

csharp

```csharp
public void SetAge(int age)
{
    if (age < 0 || age > 120)
    {
        throw new InvalidAgeException($"Age {age} is invalid.
Must be between 0 and 120.");
    }
}
```

If the supplied age is out of the valid range, the custom exception is thrown with a descriptive message.

Handling Custom Exceptions

Handling custom exceptions follows the same pattern as predefined exceptions.

csharp

```csharp
try
{
    SetAge(-5);
}
catch (InvalidAgeException ex)
{
    Console.WriteLine($"Error: {ex.Message}");
}
```

The exception is caught and an appropriate message is displayed.

Best Error-Handling Practices

Adopting best practices in error handling improves code reliability and maintainability.

Avoid Unnecessary Exceptions

Exceptions should be used for unexpected conditions, not for normal control flow. Validate inputs before performing operations to avoid unnecessary exceptions.

csharp

```csharp
if (age >= 0 && age <= 120)
{
    SetAge(age);
}
else
{
    Console.WriteLine("Invalid age provided.");
}
```

Catch Only Relevant Exceptions

Catching generic exceptions like Exception can mask real problems. Whenever possible, specify the exact type of exception to be handled.

csharp

```csharp
try
```

```csharp
{
    ProcessData();
}
catch (IOException ex)
{
    Console.WriteLine($"I/O error: {ex.Message}");
}
catch (UnauthorizedAccessException ex)
{
    Console.WriteLine("Access denied.");
}
```

This approach allows handling different types of errors appropriately.

Reuse Inner Exceptions

When creating custom exceptions, reusing inner exceptions provides more context about the original error.

csharp

```csharp
try
{
    SaveData();
}
catch (IOException ex)
{
    throw new CustomSaveException("Failed to save data.", ex);
```

}

The CustomSaveException encapsulates the original exception, preserving useful debugging information.

Error Logging

Logging exceptions is crucial for monitoring and debugging applications. Libraries such as Serilog and NLog offer robust logging solutions.

csharp

```csharp
try
{
    OpenDatabaseConnection();
}
catch (Exception ex)
{
    Log.Error(ex, "An error occurred while opening the database connection.");
    throw;
}
```

Logs provide insights about failures without interrupting program execution.

Ensuring Resource Release

Using the finally block or the using statement ensures that resources such as files and connections are released correctly.

csharp

```
using (SqlConnection connection = new
SqlConnection(connectionString))
{
    connection.Open();
    // Database operations
}
```

The using statement automatically releases the resource at the end of the block, even if an exception occurs.

Documenting Exceptions

Documenting expected exceptions in methods helps other developers understand how to handle possible errors.

csharp

```
/// <summary>
/// Sets the age of the person.
/// </summary>
/// <param name="age">The age to set.</param>
/// <exception cref="InvalidAgeException">Thrown when the age is less than 0 or greater than 120.</exception>
public void SetAge(int age)
{
    if (age < 0 || age > 120)
    {
```

```
        throw new InvalidAgeException();

    }

}
```

Documentation clarifies under which conditions an exception may be thrown.

Combining Concepts

Integrating the presented practices and concepts results in more resilient and secure code.

csharp

```csharp
public void ProcessFile(string filePath)

{

    if (string.IsNullOrEmpty(filePath))

    {

        throw new ArgumentException("File path cannot be null or empty.", nameof(filePath));

    }


    try

    {

        using (StreamReader reader = new StreamReader(filePath))

        {

            string content = reader.ReadToEnd();

            Console.WriteLine(content);
```

```
        }
    }
    catch (FileNotFoundException ex)
    {
        Console.WriteLine("The specified file does not exist.");
        Log.Error(ex, "File not found.");
    }
    catch (IOException ex)
    {
        Console.WriteLine("An error occurred while reading the file.");
        Log.Error(ex, "I/O error.");
    }
    catch (Exception ex)
    {
        Console.WriteLine("An unexpected error occurred.");
        Log.Error(ex, "Unexpected error.");
        throw;
    }
    finally
    {
        Console.WriteLine("File processing complete.");
    }
}
```

The `ProcessFile` method validates the file path, reads the content, and handles possible errors, ensuring the program remains stable even in adverse conditions.

Common Error Resolution

Error: Failure to catch specific exceptions.
Solution: Always catch concrete types such as IOException or FormatException instead of generic Exception.

Error: Loss of information from the original exception.
Solution: When rethrowing an exception, use throw; without arguments to preserve the stack trace.

Error: Resources not released after an error.
Solution: Use finally or the using statement to ensure automatic resource release.

Best Practices

- Validate data before executing operations that may cause predictable errors.

- Log error messages in centralized logs with contextual details.

- Keep exception messages clear, without exposing sensitive information.

Strategic Summary

Exception handling in C# keeps control over execution even in the face of failures. Proper use of try, catch, and finally preserves stability, while custom exceptions allow you to identify specific causes. Validating inputs, catching only relevant errors, and logging occurrences ensure reliability, reduce the impact of failures, and simplify maintenance.

CHAPTER 11. WORKING WITH FILES

File handling is an indispensable skill in software development. In C#, you can easily perform file reading, writing, and processing operations using the classes and methods provided by the .NET library. This chapter explores the fundamental techniques for reading and writing files, stream and binary file handling, and serialization/deserialization of data for efficient persistence and retrieval of information.

Reading and Writing Files

Writing to Text Files:

The StreamWriter class allows you to write data to text files. If the file does not exist, it is created automatically.

csharp

```csharp
using System.IO;

string filePath = "example.txt";

using (StreamWriter writer = new StreamWriter(filePath))
{
    writer.WriteLine("Hello, World!");
    writer.WriteLine("Welcome to file handling in C#.");
```

```
}
```

The WriteLine method adds a line to the file, and the using block ensures the resource is released properly.

Reading Text Files:

The StreamReader class enables efficient reading of text file content.

csharp

```
using (StreamReader reader = new StreamReader(filePath))
{
    string content = reader.ReadToEnd();
    Console.WriteLine(content);
}
```

The ReadToEnd method reads the entire content of the file and returns it as a single string.

Simple Read/Write with File and FileInfo:

The File and FileInfo classes provide simple methods for writing and reading, ideal for small files.

csharp

```
string content = "Quick write and read example.";
File.WriteAllText("quick_example.txt", content);

string readContent = File.ReadAllText("quick_example.txt");
Console.WriteLine(readContent);
```

The WriteAllText and ReadAllText methods allow direct manipulation of text files, simplifying common operations.

Stream Handling

Streams provide a flexible and efficient way to read and write data to files, regardless of the format.

Handling Binary Files

Binary files store data in raw format, requiring reading and writing byte by byte. The FileStream and BinaryWriter classes are useful in this context.

csharp

```csharp
using (FileStream fs = new FileStream("binary_example.bin",
FileMode.Create))
{
    using (BinaryWriter writer = new BinaryWriter(fs))
    {
        writer.Write(42);       // Writes an integer
        writer.Write(3.14);     // Writes a floating-point number
        writer.Write("Hello");  // Writes a string
    }
}
```

The Write method of the BinaryWriter class allows writing different data types to the file.

Reading Binary Files

To read binary data, use the BinaryReader class.

csharp

```
using (FileStream fs = new FileStream("binary_example.bin",
FileMode.Open))
{
    using (BinaryReader reader = new BinaryReader(fs))
    {
        int number = reader.ReadInt32();
        double pi = reader.ReadDouble();
        string message = reader.ReadString();

        Console.WriteLine($"Number: {number}, Pi: {pi}, Message:
{message}");
    }
}
```

Methods like ReadInt32, ReadDouble, and ReadString read data according to the expected type.

Memory Streams

The MemoryStream and BufferedStream classes allow data to be manipulated in memory before being persisted to files, optimizing operations.

csharp

```csharp
byte[] buffer = new byte[256];

using (MemoryStream ms = new MemoryStream(buffer))
{
    ms.WriteByte(65); // Writes the byte corresponding to 'A'
}


Console.WriteLine(System.Text.Encoding.UTF8.GetString(buffe
r));
```

Combining MemoryStream with encoding makes it easy to manipulate strings as data streams.

Serialization and Deserialization

Serialization converts objects into a format that can be stored or transmitted, while deserialization reverses this process, reconstructing the object.

JSON Serialization

JSON serialization is widely used for its compatibility with various platforms. The System.Text.Json library provides efficient methods for this purpose.

csharp

```csharp
using System.Text.Json;


public class Person
```

```csharp
{
    public string Name { get; set; }
    public int Age { get; set; }
}


Person person = new Person { Name = "Alice", Age = 30 };
string json = JsonSerializer.Serialize(person);


File.WriteAllText("person.json", json);
Console.WriteLine(json);
```

The Serialize method converts the object into a JSON string, which can be written to a file.

JSON Deserialization

Deserialization reconstructs the original object from JSON.

csharp

```csharp
string jsonContent = File.ReadAllText("person.json");
Person deserializedPerson =
JsonSerializer.Deserialize<Person>(jsonContent);


Console.WriteLine($"Name: {deserializedPerson.Name}, Age:
{deserializedPerson.Age}");
```

The Deserialize method recreates the original object based on the JSON string.

Binary Serialization

Binary serialization is useful for storing objects in a compact format, though it is less portable than JSON.

csharp

```
using System.Runtime.Serialization.Formatters.Binary;


[Serializable]
public class Product
{
    public string Name { get; set; }
    public decimal Price { get; set; }
}


Product product = new Product { Name = "Laptop", Price =
999.99m };


using (FileStream fs = new FileStream("product.bin",
FileMode.Create))
{
    BinaryFormatter formatter = new BinaryFormatter();
    formatter.Serialize(fs, product);
}
```

The [Serializable] attribute indicates that the class can be serialized.

Binary Deserialization

Binary deserialization reconstructs previously serialized objects.

csharp

```
using (FileStream fs = new FileStream("product.bin",
FileMode.Open))
{
    BinaryFormatter formatter = new BinaryFormatter();
    Product deserializedProduct =
(Product)formatter.Deserialize(fs);


    Console.WriteLine($"Name: {deserializedProduct.Name},
Price: {deserializedProduct.Price}");
}
```

The binary data from the file is converted back into the Product object.

Best Practices for File Handling

Use Using Blocks

Always release resources such as streams after use to prevent memory leaks and file errors.

Handle Exceptions

File operations are prone to errors, such as missing files or insufficient permissions. Handling exceptions ensures that the application remains stable.

csharp

```
try
{
    string content = File.ReadAllText("nonexistent.txt");
}
catch (FileNotFoundException ex)
{
    Console.WriteLine("File not found.");
}
```

Validate Inputs

Before accessing files, check the validity of the path and file existence to reduce errors.

csharp

```
if (File.Exists("data.txt"))
{
    string data = File.ReadAllText("data.txt");
}
else
{
    Console.WriteLine("File does not exist.");
}
```

Avoid Concurrency Conflicts

To avoid simultaneous access to the same file, use locks or asynchronous methods.

csharp

```
using (FileStream fs = new FileStream("shared.txt",
FileMode.OpenOrCreate, FileAccess.ReadWrite,
FileShare.None))
{
    // Safe operations on shared files
}
```

Prioritize Portable Formats

Whenever possible, use widely supported formats like JSON or XML to maximize compatibility.

Common Error Resolution

Error: File not found during reading.
Solution: Before opening a file, check its existence with File.Exists(path) to avoid FileNotFoundException.

Error: Failure to access a file in use by another process.
Solution: Use FileShare.ReadWrite in the FileStream constructor or implement concurrency control with access locks.

Error: Serialization fails because the class is not marked as serializable.
Solution: Add the [Serializable] attribute or configure the type for JSON with valid public properties.

Best Practices

- Always use using blocks to ensure streams are closed.

- Handle I/O exceptions individually to identify the real cause of the error.

- Prefer portable formats like JSON for durable and compatible data persistence.

Strategic Summary

File operations in C# require strict control over reading, writing, and resource release. Using StreamReader, StreamWriter, and binary streams allows for predictable and safe data handling. Serialization and deserialization transform objects into permanent formats, facilitating storage and transport of information. Careful management of these resources ensures data integrity and system stability in any execution environment.

CHAPTER 12. ASYNCHRONOUS PROGRAMMING WITH C#

Asynchronous programming is a powerful approach to improving the performance and responsiveness of modern applications. In C#, asynchronous programming concepts are widely implemented using async and await, which simplify the management of operations that may take time, such as database access, external API calls, and file handling. In this chapter, we cover the fundamentals of async/await, task management, and multithreading, along with real-world use cases for asynchronous operations.

Introduction to async/await

The asynchronous programming model in C# uses keywords that make code more readable and maintainable, eliminating the complexity of traditional callback-based approaches.

The async Keyword

A method is marked as async to indicate that it may contain asynchronous operations. Asynchronous methods return a Task or Task<T>, except when no value is to be returned, in which case the return type is void (only for event handlers).

csharp

```
public async Task DoSomethingAsync()
{
    await Task.Delay(1000); // Simulates an asynchronous
```

operation

    Console.WriteLine("Operation completed.");

}

The method above executes asynchronously and uses Task.Delay to simulate a 1-second pause.

The await Keyword

await is used to await the completion of an asynchronous operation before continuing the execution of subsequent code.

csharp

```
public async Task ExecuteAsync()
{
    Console.WriteLine("Starting operation...");
    await Task.Delay(2000); // Waits for the operation to finish
    Console.WriteLine("Operation finished.");
}
```

Using await frees the current thread to perform other tasks while waiting for the operation to complete.

Difference Between Synchronous and Asynchronous Methods

Synchronous methods block the main thread while waiting for a task to complete. In contrast, asynchronous methods allow other operations to continue while waiting.

csharp

```
// Synchronous method
```

```csharp
public void PerformSync()
{
    Thread.Sleep(3000);
    Console.WriteLine("Synchronous operation completed.");
}


// Asynchronous method
public async Task PerformAsync()
{
    await Task.Delay(3000);
    Console.WriteLine("Asynchronous operation completed.");
}
```

In the synchronous method, program execution is blocked during the pause, while in the asynchronous method, the program remains responsive.

Task Management and Multithreading

The Task Class

The Task class represents an asynchronous operation and is the foundation of the asynchronous programming model in C#. It enables you to create, execute, and monitor tasks.

csharp

```csharp
public async Task<string> FetchDataAsync()
{
```

```
await Task.Delay(1000); // Simulates latency
return "Data fetched successfully.";
}
```

The method returns a `Task<string>`, allowing the caller to get the result as soon as the operation completes.

Creating and Running Tasks

Tasks can be explicitly created and executed using `Task.Run`.

csharp

```
Task<int> computeTask = Task.Run(() =>
{
    int result = 0;
    for (int i = 1; i <= 10; i++)
    {
        result += i;
    }
    return result;
});


int sum = await computeTask;
Console.WriteLine($"Sum: {sum}");
```

The task runs on a separate thread while the main program continues execution.

Parallelism with Multiple Tasks

The Task.WhenAll method allows you to execute multiple tasks simultaneously and wait for all to complete.

csharp

```csharp
public async Task ProcessMultipleTasksAsync()
{
    Task task1 = Task.Delay(2000);
    Task task2 = Task.Delay(3000);
    Task task3 = Task.Delay(1000);

    await Task.WhenAll(task1, task2, task3);
    Console.WriteLine("All tasks completed.");
}
```

The three tasks start simultaneously, and the method waits for all to finish before proceeding.

Task Cancellation

The CancellationToken class allows tasks to be cancelled in a controlled way.

csharp

```csharp
public async Task PerformCancellableTask(CancellationToken cancellationToken)
{
    for (int i = 0; i < 10; i++)
```

```
{
    if (cancellationToken.IsCancellationRequested)
    {
        Console.WriteLine("Task was cancelled.");
        return;
    }
    await Task.Delay(1000);
    Console.WriteLine($"Iteration {i + 1} completed.");
    }
}
```

The cancellation token enables safe interruption of the task while preserving application state.

Multithreading and Synchronization

Although asynchronous programming simplifies many operations, understanding how threads work is important to maximize performance in advanced scenarios.

The Thread Class

The Thread class is used to explicitly create and manage threads.

csharp

```
Thread thread = new Thread(() =>
{
```

```csharp
    for (int i = 0; i < 5; i++)
    {
        Console.WriteLine($"Thread: {i}");
        Thread.Sleep(500);
    }
});


thread.Start();
```

The `Start` method begins thread execution, which operates independently of the main flow.

Synchronization with lock

Synchronization avoids race conditions in scenarios where multiple threads access shared resources.

csharp

```csharp
private static readonly object _lock = new object();
private static int _counter = 0;


public static void IncrementCounter()
{
    lock (_lock)
    {
        _counter++;
        Console.WriteLine($"Counter: {_counter}");
```

```
    }
}
```

The lock block ensures that only one thread at a time accesses the protected resource.

Use Cases for Asynchronous Operations

Calling External APIs

Asynchronous programming is widely used to consume REST APIs without blocking the main flow.

csharp

```
using System.Net.Http;

public async Task FetchApiDataAsync()
{
    using HttpClient client = new HttpClient();
    string data = await client.GetStringAsync("https://
api.example.com/data");
    Console.WriteLine(data);
}
```

Using HttpClient with await allows the application to remain responsive during the request.

Reading and Writing Files

File operations can be optimized using asynchronous methods like File.ReadAllTextAsync.

csharp

```
string content = await File.ReadAllTextAsync("largefile.txt");
Console.WriteLine(content);
```

Asynchronous reading avoids blocking during processing of large files.

Responsive Interface

In desktop or mobile applications, long-running operations can be performed asynchronously to prevent the UI from freezing.

csharp

```
public async Task PerformLengthyOperationAsync()
{
    await Task.Delay(5000);
    Console.WriteLine("Operation completed.");
}
```

This approach greatly improves user experience by keeping the interface interactive.

Batch Data Processing

Batch processing can be divided into parallel tasks to better leverage system resources.

csharp

```
List<int> data = Enumerable.Range(1, 1000).ToList();

await Task.WhenAll(data.Select(async number =>
{
    await Task.Delay(10); // Simulates processing
    Console.WriteLine($"Processed: {number}");
}));
```

Tasks are executed in parallel, reducing total processing time.

Common Error Resolution

Error: Incorrect use of await in methods not marked as async.
Solution: Add the async modifier to the method signature to allow use of await.

Error: Thread blocking when using .Result or .Wait().
Solution: Avoid synchronous calls in asynchronous tasks; use await to avoid blocking execution.

Error: Ignored task cancellation.
Solution: Check cancellationToken.IsCancellationRequested periodically within the method and exit execution when requested.

Best Practices

- Use ConfigureAwait(false) in libraries and methods that do not depend on the UI context.

- Prefer Task.WhenAll and Task.WhenAny for coordinating multiple tasks.

- Use HttpClient as a reusable instance to avoid socket exhaustion.

Strategic Summary

Asynchronous execution in C# allows long-running operations to occur without interrupting the main flow, keeping the system responsive. The combination of async and await organizes tasks clearly, avoids unnecessary blocking, and better distributes processing among threads. This model improves performance in network operations, file access, and parallel processes, ensuring fast responses and stable execution even under high load.

CHAPTER 13. LINQ: LANGUAGE INTEGRATED QUERY

Language Integrated Query (LINQ) is one of the most powerful features of C#. It allows you to perform queries against data collections, databases, XML, and other data sources in an intuitive way, using a unified and fluent syntax. This chapter covers the fundamentals of LINQ, its benefits, examples of simple and advanced queries, and the use of operators for efficient data manipulation.

Fundamentals and Benefits of LINQ

LINQ is an abstraction that unifies how developers query data. It eliminates the need for specialized languages to access different data types, such as SQL for databases and XPath for XML. Instead, all queries are written directly in C#.

LINQ Components

LINQ consists of three main components:

- **Data Sources:** Collections, databases, XML files, etc.

- **Query Operators:** Methods used to manipulate and query data.

- **Query Execution:** Results can be executed immediately or deferred.

Benefits of LINQ

- **Consistency:** A single syntax for different data sources.

- **Readability:** Queries are written in C#, eliminating the need for complex strings.

- **Type Safety:** The compiler checks queries, reducing errors.

- **Productivity:** Predefined operators simplify common tasks.

Simple and Advanced Queries

Queries on Collections

LINQ can be used to query collections like lists and arrays. The query syntax is declarative, similar to SQL.

csharp

```
List<int> numbers = new List<int> { 1, 2, 3, 4, 5, 6, 7, 8, 9, 10 };

var evenNumbers = from number in numbers
           where number % 2 == 0
           select number;

foreach (var num in evenNumbers)
{
    Console.WriteLine(num);
}
```

The above query returns all even numbers from the list. The where keyword filters the data, and select defines what will be returned.

Method Syntax Queries

Besides declarative syntax, LINQ supports a method-based syntax using extension methods.

csharp

```
var evenNumbers = numbers.Where(n => n % 2 == 0);
evenNumbers.ToList().ForEach(Console.WriteLine);
```

Method syntax is widely used for its clarity and conciseness.

Advanced Queries

Queries can be combined for more complex operations such as sorting, grouping, and data projection.

Sorting

The orderby operator sorts results in ascending or descending order.

csharp

```
var orderedNumbers = from number in numbers
                     where number > 3
                     orderby number descending
                     select number;
```

```
orderedNumbers.ToList().ForEach(Console.WriteLine);
```

Grouping

The group operator groups elements based on a key.

csharp

```
var groupedNumbers = from number in numbers
                group number by number % 2 into groups
                select new { Key = groups.Key, Values = groups };


foreach (var group in groupedNumbers)
{
    Console.WriteLine($"Group: {group.Key}");
    foreach (var value in group.Values)
    {
        Console.WriteLine($" Value: {value}");
    }
}
```

Projection

Projection creates new objects from the query results.

csharp

```
var projections = from number in numbers
            select new { Number = number, Square = number *
number };
```

```csharp
foreach (var item in projections)
{
    Console.WriteLine($"Number: {item.Number}, Square: {item.Square}");
}
```

Database Queries

LINQ to SQL and Entity Framework allow LINQ queries to be translated into SQL commands and executed directly in the database.

Configuration

Entity Framework Core is widely used for LINQ queries against databases. First, a context class is configured to represent the database.

csharp

```csharp
public class ApplicationContext : DbContext
{
    public DbSet<Product> Products { get; set; }


    protected override void OnConfiguring(DbContextOptionsBuilder options)
    {
        options.UseSqlServer("your_connection_string");
    }
}
```

```csharp
public class Product
{
    public int Id { get; set; }
    public string Name { get; set; }
    public decimal Price { get; set; }
}
```

Database Queries

Once configured, the context allows you to perform LINQ queries directly.

csharp

```csharp
using (var context = new ApplicationContext())
{
    var expensiveProducts = from product in context.Products
                where product.Price > 100
                select product;

    foreach (var product in expensiveProducts)
    {
        Console.WriteLine($"{product.Name}: {product.Price}");
    }
}
```

The above model returns all products with a price greater than

100.

Working with LINQ Operators

Filtering Operators

- **Where:** Filters elements based on a condition.

csharp
```
var filtered = numbers.Where(n => n > 5);
```

- **Take and Skip:** Return a portion of the collection.

csharp
```
var firstThree = numbers.Take(3);
var skipThree = numbers.Skip(3);
```

Projection Operators

- **Select:** Transforms the elements of the collection.

csharp
```
var squares = numbers.Select(n => n * n);
```

- **SelectMany:** Works with nested collections.

csharp
```
var nestedNumbers = new List<List<int>>
{
```

```
    new List<int> { 1, 2, 3 },
    new List<int> { 4, 5, 6 }
};
```

```
var flattened = nestedNumbers.SelectMany(list => list);
flattened.ToList().ForEach(Console.WriteLine);
```

Sorting Operators

- **OrderBy and OrderByDescending:** Sort elements.

csharp
```
var descending = numbers.OrderByDescending(n => n);
```

Set Operators

- **Distinct:** Removes duplicates.

csharp
```
var distinctNumbers = numbers.Distinct();
```

- **Union, Intersect, Except:** Perform set operations.

csharp
```
var set1 = new List<int> { 1, 2, 3 };
var set2 = new List<int> { 3, 4, 5 };
```

```
var union = set1.Union(set2);

var intersect = set1.Intersect(set2);

var except = set1.Except(set2);
```

Grouping and Aggregation Operators

- **GroupBy:** Groups elements.

csharp

```
var grouped = numbers.GroupBy(n => n % 2);
```

- **Sum, Average, Count:** Perform aggregate operations.

csharp

```
var total = numbers.Sum();

var average = numbers.Average();

var count = numbers.Count();
```

Common Error Resolution

Error: Premature execution of LINQ queries.
Solution: Remember that LINQ queries use deferred execution; use ToList() or ToArray() when you need to materialize the results immediately.

Error: Modifying a collection during LINQ iteration.
Solution: Create a new list from the result (.ToList()) before modifying the original collection.

Error: Exceptions in database queries via LINQ to SQL.

Solution: Validate the connection and check if the expression can be translated into SQL before execution.

Best Practices

- Prefer method syntax for short, chained expressions.

- Use Select and Where in logical sequence, filtering before projecting results.

- Avoid complex nested queries; break steps apart to improve clarity and performance.

Strategic Summary

LINQ unifies data access in C#, enabling expressive queries over collections, databases, and diverse structures with a coherent syntax. The combination of operators such as Where, Select, GroupBy, and OrderBy eliminates repetitive code and enhances readability. This model integrates declarative logic into functional code, reducing errors, increasing consistency, and offering precise control over filtering, projection, and aggregation of information.

CHAPTER 14. WINDOWS FORMS DEVELOPMENT

Windows Forms is one of the oldest and most stable technologies in the .NET platform for creating graphical user interfaces (GUIs) on Windows applications. Despite newer technologies like WPF and .NET MAUI, Windows Forms remains widely used due to its simplicity and efficiency. This chapter details creating basic graphical interfaces, handling events and visual elements, and connecting forms to business logic.

Creating Basic Graphical Interfaces

A Windows Forms application begins with creating forms, which serve as the main interface for the user. Each form is a window that can contain buttons, text boxes, labels, and other visual elements.

Project Setup

To create a Windows Forms application, first set up a project in Visual Studio:

1. In the main menu, choose File > New > Project.

2. Select Windows Forms App (.NET) and click Next.

3. Enter the project name and location, then click Create.

Visual Studio automatically creates a Form1.cs file, which is the application's initial form.

Adding Visual Elements

Visual elements can be added by dragging controls from the Toolbox to the form.

1. Add a Button and a Label to the form.

2. Change the controls' properties in the Properties window:

   o   Set the button text to "Click Here".

   o   Name the label lblMessage.

Form Code

The Form1.Designer.cs file contains the automatically generated code for the added controls. The main Form1.cs file contains your logic and event handlers.

csharp

```csharp
public partial class Form1 : Form
{
    public Form1()
    {
        InitializeComponent();
    }

    private void btnClick_Click(object sender, EventArgs e)
    {
        lblMessage.Text = "Button clicked!";
    }
}
```

In this example, the btnClick_Click method is linked to the button's Click event. When the button is clicked, the label's text is updated.

Events and Handling Visual Elements

Event-driven programming is central to Windows Forms development. Events allow you to respond to user actions like clicks, key presses, and mouse movement.

Handling Events

Events are handled by associating methods to controls in the form. Visual Studio makes this easy through the Events (lightning bolt) tab in Properties:

1. Click the button in the form.

2. Go to the events tab and double-click the Click event.

3. Visual Studio creates an empty method for you to implement your logic.

csharp

```
private void btnSubmit_Click(object sender, EventArgs e)
{
    MessageBox.Show("Form submitted successfully!");
}
```

Manipulating Controls at Runtime

Controls can be created and manipulated dynamically in code.

csharp

```csharp
Button dynamicButton = new Button();
dynamicButton.Text = "Dynamic";
dynamicButton.Location = new Point(50, 50);
dynamicButton.Click += DynamicButton_Click;
this.Controls.Add(dynamicButton);

private void DynamicButton_Click(object sender, EventArgs e)
{
    MessageBox.Show("Dynamic button clicked!");
}
```

Layout and Organization

Layout can be managed manually or by using containers like FlowLayoutPanel and TableLayoutPanel.

csharp

```csharp
FlowLayoutPanel flowLayout = new FlowLayoutPanel();
flowLayout.Dock = DockStyle.Fill;

Button btn1 = new Button { Text = "Button 1" };
Button btn2 = new Button { Text = "Button 2" };

flowLayout.Controls.Add(btn1);
flowLayout.Controls.Add(btn2);
```

```csharp
this.Controls.Add(flowLayout);
```

FlowLayoutPanel organizes added controls automatically, saving effort on manual positioning.

Connecting Forms to Business Logic

A real application usually requires integrating forms with business logic for processing data and executing actions.

Using Business Layers

Split the application into layers to separate the user interface from business logic.

1. Create a class in a separate file to encapsulate business logic.

csharp

```csharp
public class BusinessLogic
{
    public string ProcessData(string input)
    {
        return $"Processed data: {input.ToUpper()}";
    }
}
```

2. In the form, instantiate the class and call its methods:

csharp

```csharp
private void btnProcess_Click(object sender, EventArgs e)
{
    BusinessLogic logic = new BusinessLogic();
    string result = logic.ProcessData(txtInput.Text);
    lblResult.Text = result;
}
```

The button calls the business logic to process the user input and displays the result.

Passing Data Between Forms

In applications with multiple forms, it's common to share data between them.

1. Create a second form (Form2) with a Label to display data.

2. In the main form, instantiate and show the second form.

csharp

```csharp
Form2 form2 = new Form2();
form2.SetMessage("Hello, Form2!");
form2.Show();
```

3. Add a method to the second form to receive data:

csharp

```csharp
public void SetMessage(string message)
```

```
{
    lblMessage.Text = message;
}
```

Database Interaction

Business logic often interacts with databases to store and retrieve information.

    1. Use SqlConnection and SqlCommand to perform operations in the database.

csharp

```
string connectionString = "your_connection_string";


using (SqlConnection connection = new
SqlConnection(connectionString))
{
    connection.Open();
    string query = "SELECT Name FROM Users WHERE Id = @Id";
    using (SqlCommand command = new SqlCommand(query,
connection))
    {
        command.Parameters.AddWithValue("@Id", 1);
        string name = command.ExecuteScalar()?.ToString();
        lblResult.Text = name;
    }
}
```

2. Connect query results to the UI, such as populating a list:

csharp

```csharp
string query = "SELECT Name FROM Users";

using (SqlCommand command = new SqlCommand(query, connection))
using (SqlDataReader reader = command.ExecuteReader())
{
    while (reader.Read())
    {
        lstUsers.Items.Add(reader["Name"].ToString());
    }
}
```

Best Practices in Windows Forms Development

Responsive Design

Avoid absolute positioning and use containers like Panel and TableLayoutPanel to create interfaces that adapt to different screen resolutions.

Input Validation

Always validate user input before processing:

csharp

```csharp
if (string.IsNullOrEmpty(txtName.Text))
{
    MessageBox.Show("The Name field is required.");
    return;
}
```

Using Threads for Long Operations

Long-running operations should be performed on separate threads to prevent UI freezing.

csharp

```csharp
private async void btnLoadData_Click(object sender, EventArgs e)
{
    lblStatus.Text = "Loading...";
    await Task.Run(() => LoadData());
    lblStatus.Text = "Completed.";
}


private void LoadData()
{
    Thread.Sleep(5000); // Simulates a long operation
}
```

Separation of Responsibilities

Keep the UI separate from business logic for easier maintenance and testing.

Exception Handling

Catch exceptions in event handlers to avoid unexpected crashes.

csharp

```
try
{
    // Potentially problematic code
}
catch (Exception ex)
{
    MessageBox.Show($"Error: {ex.Message}");
}
```

Common Error Resolution

Error: UI freezes during long operation.
Solution: Run intensive tasks with Task.Run() or BackgroundWorker to keep the interface responsive.

Error: Unhandled exceptions in events.
Solution: Wrap event logic in try-catch blocks to catch errors and show friendly messages.

Error: Failing to access controls from another thread.
Solution: Use Invoke() or BeginInvoke() to update UI elements from background threads.

Best Practices

- Separate business logic from the UI, keeping forms only for user interaction.

- Validate all inputs before processing data.

- Use layout containers to automatically adjust the interface to different resolutions.

Strategic Summary

Windows Forms provides a solid foundation for building desktop interfaces in C#. The event model simplifies user-system interaction, while integration with business logic enables automation and direct processing. The use of asynchronous threads, exception handling, and responsive design ensures stable performance, simple maintenance, and a smooth experience in enterprise applications.

CHAPTER 15. WEB DEVELOPMENT WITH ASP.NET

ASP.NET is one of Microsoft's main technologies for developing modern web applications. It supports different paradigms, such as MVC (Model-View-Controller), which facilitates the construction of modular and scalable applications. Additionally, ASP.NET enables the creation of robust RESTful APIs, integrating seamlessly into the .NET ecosystem. In this chapter, we will explore the fundamentals of ASP.NET, building basic web applications, and implementing RESTful APIs using C#.

Fundamentals of ASP.NET and MVC

ASP.NET is a development platform that allows you to create dynamic web applications. It supports both page-based approaches (Web Forms) and the MVC architecture, which is widely used in modern projects.

Main Components of ASP.NET MVC

The MVC pattern divides the application into three main components:

1. **Model:** Represents the application's data logic. It is usually associated with a database and contains classes representing data and their operations.

2. **View:** Responsible for the user interface, displaying information to users and collecting input.

3. **Controller:** Manages the interaction between the user,

the model, and the views. It processes user input, updates the model, and selects the appropriate view.

Lifecycle of an ASP.NET MVC Request

When a request reaches an ASP.NET MVC application, the flow is divided into several steps:

1. **Routing:** Determines which controller and action should be executed based on the URL.

2. **Controller:** Processes business logic and collects data from the model.

3. **View:** Renders the data and displays it to the user.

Project Configuration

In Visual Studio, create a new ASP.NET Core MVC project:

1. Go to File > New > Project.

2. Select ASP.NET Core Web Application (MVC Model).

3. Set the project name and location and click Create.

The generated project includes a basic structure with directories like Controllers, Models, and Views, reflecting the MVC pattern.

Building Basic Web Applications

Models

Models represent data and business logic. They are defined as classes in the Models directory.

csharp

```csharp
public class Product
{
    public int Id { get; set; }
    public string Name { get; set; }
    public decimal Price { get; set; }
}
```

Controllers

Controllers handle requests and return responses. A basic controller can be created in Controllers.

csharp

```csharp
using Microsoft.AspNetCore.Mvc;

public class ProductController : Controller
{
    public IActionResult Index()
    {
        var products = new List<Product>
        {
            new Product { Id = 1, Name = "Laptop", Price = 1500 },
            new Product { Id = 2, Name = "Smartphone", Price = 800 }
        };

        return View(products);
```

```
    }
}
```

The Index method returns a list of products that will be displayed in the corresponding view.

Views

Views are created in the Views directory. In the example above, a view for the Index method should be created in Views/Product/Index.cshtml.

html

```
@model IEnumerable<Product>


<h2>Product List</h2>
<table>
    <thead>
        <tr>
            <th>Id</th>
            <th>Name</th>
            <th>Price</th>
        </tr>
    </thead>
    <tbody>
        @foreach (var product in Model)
        {
            <tr>
```

```
            <td>@product.Id</td>
            <td>@product.Name</td>
            <td>@product.Price</td>
        </tr>
    }
    </tbody>
</table>
```

The @model directive specifies the data type the view receives, while Razor code displays the products in a table.

Routing

Routing is configured in the Program.cs file. The default route maps URLs to controllers and actions.

csharp

```
app.MapControllerRoute(
    name: "default",
    pattern: "{controller=Home}/{action=Index}/{id?}");
```

The default route points to the Home controller and the Index action.

Implementing RESTful APIs with C#

Basic API Structure

A RESTful API allows different systems to interact through HTTP requests. ASP.NET simplifies API creation with specific controllers.

Create a controller in the Controllers folder:

csharp

```
using Microsoft.AspNetCore.Mvc;


[ApiController]
[Route("api/[controller]")]
public class ProductsController : ControllerBase
{
    private static readonly List<Product> Products = new
List<Product>
    {
        new Product { Id = 1, Name = "Laptop", Price = 1500 },
        new Product { Id = 2, Name = "Smartphone", Price = 800 }
    };


    [HttpGet]
    public IActionResult GetAll()
    {
        return Ok(Products);
    }


    [HttpGet("{id}")]
    public IActionResult GetById(int id)
```

```csharp
    {
        var product = Products.FirstOrDefault(p => p.Id == id);
        if (product == null) return NotFound();


        return Ok(product);
    }


    [HttpPost]
    public IActionResult Create(Product product)
    {
        Products.Add(product);
        return CreatedAtAction(nameof(GetById), new { id =
product.Id }, product);
    }


    [HttpDelete("{id}")]
    public IActionResult Delete(int id)
    {
        var product = Products.FirstOrDefault(p => p.Id == id);
        if (product == null) return NotFound();


        Products.Remove(product);
        return NoContent();
    }
}
```

Testing the API

Use tools like Postman or Swagger (integrated with ASP.NET) to test endpoints.

1. In Program.cs, add support for Swagger:

csharp

```
app.UseSwagger();
app.UseSwaggerUI();
```

2. Start the application and access /swagger in the browser to explore the endpoints.

Data Validation

Add validations to models to ensure submitted data meets specific criteria.

csharp

```
using System.ComponentModel.DataAnnotations;


public class Product
{
    public int Id { get; set; }

    [Required]
    [StringLength(50)]
    public string Name { get; set; }
```

```
[Range(0, 10000)]
public decimal Price { get; set; }
}
```

In the controller, validate the model before processing the request:

csharp

```
[HttpPost]
public IActionResult Create([FromBody] Product product)
{
    if (!ModelState.IsValid) return BadRequest(ModelState);

    Products.Add(product);
    return CreatedAtAction(nameof(GetById), new { id = product.Id }, product);
}
```

Connecting to Databases

Configuring Entity Framework Core

Add support for Entity Framework to handle databases.

     1. Configure the context in Program.cs:

csharp

```
builder.Services.AddDbContext<ApplicationDbContext>(options =>
    options.UseSqlServer("your_connection_string"));
```

2. **Create the context and entities:**

csharp

```
using Microsoft.EntityFrameworkCore;

public class ApplicationDbContext : DbContext
{
    public DbSet<Product> Products { get; set; }

    public ApplicationDbContext(DbContextOptions<ApplicationDbContext> options) : base(options) { }
}
```

3. **Run migrations to create the table in the database:**

bash

```
dotnet ef migrations add InitialCreate
dotnet ef database update
```

Querying Data

Update the controller to interact with the database:

csharp

```csharp
private readonly ApplicationDbContext _context;


public ProductsController(ApplicationDbContext context)
{
    _context = context;
}


[HttpGet]
public IActionResult GetAll()
{
    return Ok(_context.Products.ToList());
}
```

Common Error Resolution

Error: Route not found when accessing a controller.
Solution: Check the route pattern defined in Program.cs and confirm that the controller and action names match the mapping.

Error: Invalid model in POST requests.
Solution: Include [ApiController] and validate ModelState before processing incoming data.

Error: Database connection failure.

Solution: Confirm the connection string and run Entity Framework migrations to create necessary tables.

Best Practices

- Separate controllers, models, and views into distinct layers to maintain the MVC pattern.

- Use validation attributes in models to prevent data inconsistencies.

- Enable Swagger in development environments to document and quickly test endpoints.

Strategic Summary

ASP.NET provides a comprehensive foundation for web development in C#, combining modular architecture, route control, and direct database integration. The MVC pattern organizes code in independent layers and makes maintenance easier, while native support for RESTful APIs enables standardized communication between systems. The described structure combines performance, security, and scalability, allowing you to build consistent and easily evolving web solutions.

CHAPTER 16. DATABASE INTEGRATION

Database integration is one of the pillars of modern application development. Databases store structured information and provide efficient means for querying and manipulating it. In this chapter, we cover how to connect C# applications to databases, perform CRUD operations (Create, Read, Update, Delete), and use Entity Framework (EF), a widely used ORM (Object-Relational Mapping) that simplifies data access.

Connecting to SQL Server and Other Databases

Configuring the Connection to SQL Server

To connect a C# application to SQL Server, use the SqlConnection class available in the System.Data.SqlClient namespace. The first step is to define the connection string, which contains information such as server name, database, credentials, and other settings.

csharp

```
string connectionString =
"Server=localhost;Database=MyDatabase;User
Id=myUser;Password=myPassword;";
```

```
using (SqlConnection connection = new
SqlConnection(connectionString))
{
    try
    {
        connection.Open();
        Console.WriteLine("Connection successful!");
    }
    catch (Exception ex)
    {
        Console.WriteLine($"Error: {ex.Message}");
    }
}
```

The connection string must be customized according to the execution environment. To prevent exposing credentials in the source code, use environment variables or a configuration file.

Connecting to Other Databases

In addition to SQL Server, C# supports integration with databases such as MySQL, PostgreSQL, and SQLite. For each of these databases, you need specific packages, which can be installed via NuGet:

- MySQL: Install MySql.Data.

- PostgreSQL: Install Npgsql.

- **SQLite: Install** System.Data.SQLite.

The connection syntax varies slightly but follows the same principle.

Example with MySQL:

csharp

```csharp
using MySql.Data.MySqlClient;


string connectionString = "Server=localhost;Database=MyDatabase;User=myUser;Password=myPassword;";
using (MySqlConnection connection = new MySqlConnection(connectionString))
{
    connection.Open();
    Console.WriteLine("Connected to MySQL!");
}
```

Example with PostgreSQL:

csharp

```csharp
using Npgsql;


string connectionString = "Host=localhost;Database=MyDatabase;Username=myUser;Password=myPassword;";
using (NpgsqlConnection connection = new NpgsqlConnection(connectionString))
```

```
{
    connection.Open();
    Console.WriteLine("Connected to PostgreSQL!");
}
```

CRUD Operations (Create, Read, Update, Delete)

CRUD operations are the core of any application that interacts with databases. They allow you to create, read, update, and delete records.

CREATE: Inserting Data

Use the SqlCommand class to execute SQL statements.

csharp

```
string insertQuery = "INSERT INTO Products (Name, Price) VALUES (@Name, @Price)";

using (SqlCommand command = new SqlCommand(insertQuery, connection))
{
    command.Parameters.AddWithValue("@Name", "Laptop");
    command.Parameters.AddWithValue("@Price", 1500);

    int rowsAffected = command.ExecuteNonQuery();
    Console.WriteLine($"{rowsAffected} row(s) inserted.");
}
```

READ: Querying Data

Use the ExecuteReader method to retrieve data.

csharp

```csharp
string selectQuery = "SELECT Id, Name, Price FROM Products";


using (SqlCommand command = new SqlCommand(selectQuery, connection))
using (SqlDataReader reader = command.ExecuteReader())
{
    while (reader.Read())
    {
        Console.WriteLine($"Id: {reader["Id"]}, Name: {reader["Name"]}, Price: {reader["Price"]}");
    }
}
```

UPDATE: Updating Data

The ExecuteNonQuery method is also used to update records.

csharp

```csharp
string updateQuery = "UPDATE Products SET Price = @Price WHERE Name = @Name";


using (SqlCommand command = new SqlCommand(updateQuery, connection))
{
```

```csharp
command.Parameters.AddWithValue("@Name", "Laptop");
command.Parameters.AddWithValue("@Price", 1700);

int rowsAffected = command.ExecuteNonQuery();
Console.WriteLine($"{rowsAffected} row(s) updated.");
}
```

DELETE: Deleting Data

Deleting records follows the same pattern.

csharp

```csharp
string deleteQuery = "DELETE FROM Products WHERE Name = @Name";

using (SqlCommand command = new SqlCommand(deleteQuery, connection))
{
    command.Parameters.AddWithValue("@Name", "Laptop");

    int rowsAffected = command.ExecuteNonQuery();
    Console.WriteLine($"{rowsAffected} row(s) deleted.");
}
```

Using ORM with Entity Framework

Entity Framework simplifies database interaction by allowing developers to work directly with C# objects instead of writing SQL queries.

Entity Framework Configuration

1. Install the NuGet package Microsoft.EntityFrameworkCore and the provider for your database (e.g., Microsoft.EntityFrameworkCore.SqlServer).
2. Set up the context and entities:

csharp

```csharp
using Microsoft.EntityFrameworkCore;


public class ApplicationDbContext : DbContext
{
    public DbSet<Product> Products { get; set; }


    protected override void OnConfiguring(DbContextOptionsBuilder options)
    {
        options.UseSqlServer("Server=localhost;Database=MyDatabase;User Id=myUser;Password=myPassword;");
    }
}
```

```csharp
public class Product
{
    public int Id { get; set; }
    public string Name { get; set; }
    public decimal Price { get; set; }
}
```

Running Migrations

Before using EF, create the database structure with migrations:

bash

```bash
dotnet ef migrations add InitialCreate
dotnet ef database update
```

Performing CRUD Operations with EF

Insert

csharp

```csharp
using (var context = new ApplicationDbContext())
{
    var product = new Product { Name = "Smartphone", Price = 800 };
    context.Products.Add(product);
    context.SaveChanges();
    Console.WriteLine("Product added.");
```

```
}
```

Query

csharp

```csharp
using (var context = new ApplicationDbContext())
{
    var products = context.Products.ToList();
    products.ForEach(p => Console.WriteLine($"{p.Name}:
{p.Price}"));
}
```

Update

csharp

```csharp
using (var context = new ApplicationDbContext())
{
    var product = context.Products.FirstOrDefault(p => p.Name
== "Smartphone");
    if (product != null)
    {
        product.Price = 850;
        context.SaveChanges();
        Console.WriteLine("Product updated.");
    }
}
```

Delete

csharp

```
using (var context = new ApplicationDbContext())
{
    var product = context.Products.FirstOrDefault(p => p.Name
== "Smartphone");
    if (product != null)
    {
        context.Products.Remove(product);
        context.SaveChanges();
        Console.WriteLine("Product deleted.");
    }
}
```

Advanced Queries

EF supports advanced queries, including filtering, sorting, and projections.

csharp

```
using (var context = new ApplicationDbContext())
{
    var filteredProducts = context.Products
        .Where(p => p.Price > 500)
        .OrderBy(p => p.Price)
        .Select(p => new { p.Name, p.Price });
```

```csharp
filteredProducts.ToList().ForEach(p =>
Console.WriteLine($"{p.Name}: {p.Price}"));
}
```

Best Practices for Database Integration

Use Transactions

Use transactions to ensure data consistency.

csharp

```csharp
using (var transaction = connection.BeginTransaction())
{
    try
    {
        // Execute commands inside the transaction
        transaction.Commit();
    }
    catch
    {
        transaction.Rollback();
    }
}
```

Avoid SQL Injection

Always use parameters instead of concatenating strings to

prevent SQL injection attacks.

Monitor Performance

Use tools like SQL Profiler to identify slow queries and optimize them.

Layer Separation

Keep data logic separate from business logic for easier maintenance and scalability.

Common Error Resolution

Error: Failed to connect to the database.
Solution: Check the connection string, access permissions, and server availability.

Error: Exception due to incorrect SQL query.
Solution: Validate SQL syntax and use parameters (AddWithValue) to prevent errors and code injection.

Error: Unmapped entities in Entity Framework.
Solution: Confirm that the DbSet was declared in the context and that migrations were applied correctly.

Best Practices

- Use parameters in all queries to prevent SQL injection attacks.

- Apply transactions (BeginTransaction) for operations involving multiple changes.

- Separate data logic from the rest of the application, adopting repositories and service layers.

Strategic Summary

Database integration in C# combines direct access via SqlClient with the abstraction of Entity Framework to simplify queries and CRUD operations. Using ORM reduces repetitive code, improves readability, and ensures data integrity. Applying transactions, validations, and well-defined layers results in stable, secure, and scalable systems ready for enterprise environments.

CHAPTER 17. GAME APPLICATIONS WITH UNITY

Unity is one of the most popular tools for game development, and C# is the main language used to create scripts and interactions in Unity. In this chapter, we cover the fundamentals of game development using C#, integrating with Unity's basic components, and creating a simple 2D game. This introduction provides the knowledge needed to build interactive and dynamic projects.

Introduction to Game Development in C#

Why Unity and C#?

Unity offers an integrated environment for creating 2D and 3D games, interactive applications, and even virtual reality experiences. C# is preferred in Unity for its simplicity, robustness, and direct integration with the Unity engine.

Benefits of Unity:

- User-friendly interface for artists and programmers.

- Cross-platform support (Windows, Android, iOS, etc.).

- Extensible, allowing the use of plugins and custom scripts.

Unity Project Structure

When creating a new project in Unity, you work with a predefined file and folder structure:

- **Assets:** Where main project files such as scripts, images, and 3D models are stored.

- **Scenes:** Contain the game layout, including object placement and specific settings.

- **Scripts:** Folders that store the C# code.

A scene is composed of GameObjects, which can have components such as transforms, renderers, and custom scripts.

Unity Basic Components and C# Scripts

GameObjects and Components

GameObjects are the fundamental building blocks in Unity. They represent objects in the game, like players, enemies, and platforms. Each GameObject can have multiple Components that define its behavior and appearance.

Example:

A "Player" GameObject can have:

- **Sprite Renderer:** Sets the visual appearance.

- **Box Collider 2D:** Enables collision detection.

- **Rigidbody 2D:** Adds physics to the object.

- **Custom Script:** Defines unique behaviors.

Creating Scripts in C#

Scripts add logic to GameObjects. To create a script:

1. Right-click the Assets folder.

2. Select Create > C# Script and give the script a name.

3. Add the script to a GameObject by dragging it onto the object in the Hierarchy.

A basic script:

csharp

```
using UnityEngine;

public class PlayerController : MonoBehaviour
{
    public float speed = 5.0f;

    void Update()
    {
        float moveHorizontal = Input.GetAxis("Horizontal");
        float moveVertical = Input.GetAxis("Vertical");

        Vector3 movement = new Vector3(moveHorizontal, moveVertical, 0.0f);
        transform.Translate(movement * speed * Time.deltaTime);
    }
}
```

In this script:

- Update is called once per frame and is used to capture player input.

- transform.Translate moves the object based on input.

Unity Events

Unity has predefined methods to respond to game events:

- **Start**: Called when the script is enabled.

- **Update**: Called every frame.

- **OnCollisionEnter2D**: Called when an object collides with another.

Collision example:

csharp

```csharp
void OnCollisionEnter2D(Collision2D collision)
{
    if (collision.gameObject.tag == "Enemy")
    {
        Debug.Log("Player hit an enemy!");
    }
}
```

This code detects a collision and checks the object's tag.

Creating a Simple 2D Game

Setting Up the Environment:

1. Open Unity and create a new 2D project.

2. In the Hierarchy panel, create these GameObjects:

   o **Player:** Add a Sprite Renderer with a character image and a Box Collider 2D.

   o **Ground:** Create a platform with a Box Collider 2D.

   o **Enemy:** Add an image for the enemy and a Rigidbody 2D.

Player Movement

Add a PlayerController script to the Player GameObject.

csharp

```csharp
using UnityEngine;

public class PlayerController : MonoBehaviour
{
    public float moveSpeed = 5f;
    private Rigidbody2D rb;

    void Start()
    {
        rb = GetComponent<Rigidbody2D>();
    }
}
```

```
void Update()
{
    float horizontal = Input.GetAxis("Horizontal");
    rb.velocity = new Vector2(horizontal * moveSpeed, rb.velocity.y);
}
}
```

This script uses a Rigidbody2D to move the player horizontally.

Adding Collision

Create a script to handle player collision with the enemy.

csharp

```
public class EnemyCollision : MonoBehaviour
{
    void OnCollisionEnter2D(Collision2D collision)
    {
    if (collision.gameObject.CompareTag("Player"))
    {
        Debug.Log("Game Over!");
    }
    }
}
```

Make sure the Player GameObject has the "Player" tag assigned.

Game Scoring

Add a scoring system. Create an empty GameObject called "GameManager" and attach this script:

csharp

```csharp
using UnityEngine;

public class GameManager : MonoBehaviour
{
    private int score = 0;

    public void AddScore(int points)
    {
        score += points;
        Debug.Log($"Score: {score}");
    }
}
```

To increase the score, add this script to the enemy:

csharp

```csharp
public class EnemyController : MonoBehaviour
{
    private GameManager gameManager;
```

```
    void Start()
    {
        gameManager = FindObjectOfType<GameManager>();
    }

    void OnDestroy()
    {
        gameManager.AddScore(10);
    }
}
```

Destroy the enemy on collision with the player or another object.

Visual Improvements and Feedback

1. Adding Animations:

Use the Animation system to create movement or event animations, such as the enemy exploding when destroyed.

2. Sound Effects:

Add audio clips to the project and play sounds during specific events.

csharp

public class SoundController : MonoBehaviour

```csharp
{
    public AudioClip hitSound;
    private AudioSource audioSource;

    void Start()
    {
        audioSource = GetComponent<AudioSource>();
    }

    void PlaySound()
    {
        audioSource.PlayOneShot(hitSound);
    }
}
```

Ending the Game

Add game-ending functionality:

csharp

```csharp
public class GameOverManager : MonoBehaviour
{
    public void GameOver()
    {
        Debug.Log("Game Over. Restarting...");
        UnityEngine.SceneManagement.SceneManager.LoadScene("MainScene");
```

```
    }
}
```

When colliding with an enemy, call the GameOver method.

Common Error Resolution

Error: The player does not move when pressing keys.
Solution: Ensure the Rigidbody2D component is attached and the "Horizontal" axis is configured in the Input Manager.

Error: Collisions are not detected.
Solution: Ensure both objects have compatible colliders and at least one has a Rigidbody2D.

Error: Score does not update.
Solution: Check if the AddScore() method is being called and if the GameManager is correctly instantiated in the scene.

Best Practices

- Organize asset folders by category (Scripts, Sprites, Audio, Scenes).

- Create Prefabs to reuse enemies, platforms, and other repetitive objects.

- Use FixedUpdate() for physics logic and Update() only for input capture.

- Apply tags and layers to facilitate collision detection and filtering.

Strategic Summary

Unity, combined with C#, offers a solid foundation for creating interactive 2D and 3D games. The combination of GameObjects, components, and scripts allows for integrated control of physics, events, and logic. With organized practices, use of prefabs, animations, and scoring systems, you can develop functional and optimized games, turning basic concepts into complete and engaging player experiences.

CHAPTER 18. SECURITY AND BEST PRACTICES

Security is a fundamental pillar in the development of any application. In an increasingly connected world, protecting systems against vulnerabilities and attacks is essential to maintain data integrity and user trust. This chapter covers input validation, prevention of common vulnerabilities, and the implementation of security standards in C# applications.

Input Validation

Input validation is the first line of defense against attacks and errors. Ensuring that only valid and expected data is processed prevents failures and protects the application from threats such as SQL injection and XSS (Cross-Site Scripting).

Fundamental Principles

1. Never trust user data: Always treat input as untrusted, even if it comes from apparently safe sources.

2. Validate on both client and server: Client-side validation improves user experience, while server-side validation is indispensable for security.

3. Specify clear rules: Use regular expressions or validation libraries to define allowed formats and values.

Implementation in C#

Validation with Regular Expressions

Regular expressions are powerful for validating specific formats, such as emails, phone numbers, or postal codes.

csharp

```csharp
using System.Text.RegularExpressions;


public bool IsValidEmail(string email)
{
    string pattern = @"^[^@\s]+@[^@\s]+\.[^@\s]+$";
    return Regex.IsMatch(email, pattern);
}
```

Type Validation

Use native C# methods to check if the input matches the expected type.

csharp

```csharp
public bool IsNumeric(string input)
{
    return int.TryParse(input, out _);
}
```

Using Validation Libraries

Libraries such as FluentValidation simplify the validation of complex objects.

csharp

```csharp
using FluentValidation;

public class User
{
    public string Name { get; set; }
    public string Email { get; set; }
}

public class UserValidator : AbstractValidator<User>
{
    public UserValidator()
    {
        RuleFor(user =>
user.Name).NotEmpty().WithMessage("Name is required.");
        RuleFor(user =>
user.Email).EmailAddress().WithMessage("Invalid email
address.");
    }
}
```

Prevention of Common Vulnerabilities

SQL Injection

SQL injection occurs when an attacker inserts malicious SQL commands into input fields. To prevent this, use parameterized queries.

csharp

```
using System.Data.SqlClient;


string query = "SELECT * FROM Users WHERE Username =
@Username AND Password = @Password";


using (SqlConnection connection = new
SqlConnection("your_connection_string"))
{
    SqlCommand command = new SqlCommand(query,
connection);
    command.Parameters.AddWithValue("@Username",
username);
    command.Parameters.AddWithValue("@Password",
password);


    connection.Open();
    SqlDataReader reader = command.ExecuteReader();
}
```

Cross-Site Scripting (XSS)

XSS occurs when malicious input is displayed without proper sanitization. Use encoding to neutralize malicious scripts.

csharp

```
using System.Web;
```

```csharp
public string SanitizeInput(string input)
{
    return HttpUtility.HtmlEncode(input);
}
```

Authentication and Session Handling

Avoid storing sensitive information, such as passwords, in plain text. Use secure hashing with salt.

csharp

```csharp
using System.Security.Cryptography;
using System.Text;


public string HashPassword(string password, string salt)
{
    using (var sha256 = SHA256.Create())
    {
        var combined = Encoding.UTF8.GetBytes(password + salt);
        return Convert.ToBase64String(sha256.ComputeHash(combined));
    }
}
```

Exposure of Sensitive Data

Never display sensitive information in error messages. Configure custom handling to show generic messages.

csharp

```csharp
try
{
    // Code that may throw exceptions
}
catch (Exception)
{
    Console.WriteLine("An error occurred. Please contact support.");
}
```

Prevention of Brute-Force Attacks

Implement a login attempt limit to prevent brute-force attacks.

csharp

```csharp
private static Dictionary<string, int> loginAttempts = new Dictionary<string, int>();

public bool IsAccountLocked(string username)
{
    return loginAttempts.ContainsKey(username) && loginAttempts[username] >= 5;
```

```csharp
}

public void RegisterFailedAttempt(string username)
{
    if (!loginAttempts.ContainsKey(username))
    {
        loginAttempts[username] = 0;
    }
    loginAttempts[username]++;
}
```

Security Standards in C# Applications

Using HTTPS

Always use HTTPS to encrypt communication between client and server. In ASP.NET Core, configure HTTPS redirection in Program.cs.

csharp

```csharp
app.UseHttpsRedirection();
```

Implementing Authentication

Use libraries such as ASP.NET Identity to manage authentication and authorization.

1. Configure the service in Program.cs:

csharp

```
builder.Services.AddIdentity<IdentityUser, IdentityRole>()
    .AddEntityFrameworkStores<ApplicationDbContext>()
    .AddDefaultTokenProviders();
```

2. Add authentication to controllers:

csharp

```
[Authorize]
public IActionResult SecurePage()
{
    return View();
}
```

CSRF Protection

CSRF tokens ensure that only valid requests are processed.

csharp

```
services.AddControllersWithViews(options =>
{
    options.Filters.Add(new
AutoValidateAntiforgeryTokenAttribute());
});
```

Include the token in the HTML generated by the server:

html

```
<form method="post" asp-antiforgery="true">
    <input type="hidden" name="__RequestVerificationToken"
```

```
value="@Antiforgery.GetTokens().RequestToken" />
</form>
```

Log Management

Log all important activities, including authentication failures and unauthorized access attempts. Use libraries such as Serilog.

csharp

```csharp
Log.Logger = new LoggerConfiguration()
    .WriteTo.Console()
    .WriteTo.File("logs.txt")
    .CreateLogger();


Log.Information("Application started.");
Log.Warning("Unauthorized access attempt.");
```

Error Monitoring

Implement systems to capture and monitor errors in real time, such as Application Insights or Sentry.

csharp

```csharp
app.UseExceptionHandler("/Home/Error");
app.UseStatusCodePagesWithReExecute("/Error/{0}");
```

Regular Updates

Keep libraries and dependencies updated to avoid known vulnerabilities. Use tools like Dependabot for automation.

Security Tool Integration

Code Analysis

Use static code analysis tools such as SonarQube to identify vulnerabilities.

Penetration Testing

Regularly perform penetration tests to identify weaknesses before they are exploited.

Supply Chain Security

Check the origin and security of dependencies used in the project. Use trusted package managers such as NuGet.

Essential Security Practices:

- Principle of Least Privilege: Grant only the necessary permissions for each resource.

- Data Sanitization: Always clean and validate user input before processing it.

- Data Encryption: Encrypt sensitive data at rest and in transit.

- Team Training: Ensure all developers understand the basic principles of security.

Common Error Resolution

Error: SQL injection in login fields.
Solution: Replace concatenated queries with parameterized

queries using SqlCommand.Parameters.AddWithValue().

Error: Sessions expiring incorrectly.
Solution: Configure authentication policies in ASP.NET Identity and consistently validate tokens.

Error: Sensitive data displayed in error messages.
Solution: Use generic messages and log details securely with tools such as Serilog.

Best Practices

- Validate all input on the server, even when client-side validation exists.

- Use HTTPS and CSRF tokens to protect communications and requests.

- Store passwords with hash and salt, avoiding any plain text.

- Log security events such as failed logins for auditing and anomaly detection.

Strategic Summary

Security in C# requires a proactive and systematic approach. Rigorous data validation, use of parameterized queries, secure authentication, and protection against attacks such as XSS, CSRF, and brute force are indispensable practices. Using HTTPS, structured logging, and continuously updating dependencies strengthen your defense against threats. By applying these guidelines, developers ensure that code is not only functional but also resilient and trustworthy in both corporate and web environments.

CHAPTER 19. TESTING AND CODE DEBUGGING

The quality of an application depends not only on its functionality but also on its reliability. Testing and debugging are crucial elements to ensure that code works as expected and to identify and fix problems. This chapter covers debugging techniques in Visual Studio, creating unit tests with NUnit, and the use of automated testing tools.

Debugging Techniques in Visual Studio

Visual Studio is one of the most advanced tools for code development and debugging. It offers a wide range of features that help developers identify issues and understand code behavior.

Using Breakpoints

Breakpoints pause program execution at specific points, allowing you to examine variables, execution flow, and values.

1. Click in the left margin of the editor next to the line where you want to pause execution.

2. Run the program in debug mode by pressing F5.

3. When the breakpoint is hit, execution pauses and you can inspect the program state.

Types of Breakpoints

- **Simple:** Pauses at the specified line.

- **Conditional:** Pauses only when a condition is true.

csharp

```csharp
int counter = 0;
for (int i = 0; i < 10; i++)
{
    counter += i; // Add a conditional breakpoint here: i == 5
}
```

- **Hit Count:** Pauses after a specific number of iterations.

Variable Inspection

Use the Locals window to view all variables available in the current scope. For specific variables, hover over the identifier or add them to the Watch window.

csharp

```csharp
int result = Calculate(5, 10); // Inspect input values and result during execution


public int Calculate(int a, int b)
{
    return a + b;
}
```

Live Debugging

During debugging, you can change variable values to test different scenarios without restarting the application.

csharp

```
int total = 100; // During debugging, change value to 200 and
observe impact on flow
```

Call Stack Tracking

The Call Stack window shows the sequence of calls leading to the current execution point, helping identify the origin of errors.

Remote Debugging

Visual Studio supports remote debugging, allowing you to analyze issues on machines without the full development environment.

1. Set up the Remote Debugging Tool on the remote machine.

2. In Visual Studio, connect to the remote process via Attach to Process.

Creating Unit Tests with NUnit

Unit tests verify the behavior of small parts of code in isolation. NUnit is one of the most popular frameworks for unit testing in C#.

Project Setup

1. Install the NUnit and NUnit3TestAdapter packages via NuGet.

2. Create a new test project in Visual Studio and reference the main project.

Unit Test Structure

A unit test in NUnit is identified by the [Test] attribute. The framework provides several helper methods for validation, such as Assert.

csharp

```csharp
using NUnit.Framework;

[TestFixture]
public class CalculatorTests
{
    [Test]
    public void Add_ShouldReturnSum_WhenInputsAreValid()
    {
        // Arrange
        var calculator = new Calculator();

        // Act
        int result = calculator.Add(2, 3);

        // Assert
        Assert.AreEqual(5, result);
    }
```

}

In this example:

- **Arrange** sets up the initial scenario.

- **Act** executes the method to be tested.

- **Assert** checks if the result is correct.

Parameterized Test Cases

Use the [TestCase] attribute to test multiple scenarios with different inputs and outputs.

csharp

```
[TestCase(2, 3, 5)]
[TestCase(-1, 1, 0)]
[TestCase(0, 0, 0)]
public void Add_ShouldReturnCorrectSum(int a, int b, int expected)
{
    var calculator = new Calculator();
    int result = calculator.Add(a, b);
    Assert.AreEqual(expected, result);
}
```

Testing Exceptions

The Assert.Throws method validates if an expected exception is thrown.

csharp

```csharp
[Test]
public void
Divide_ShouldThrowException_WhenDividingByZero()
{
    var calculator = new Calculator();
    Assert.Throws<DivideByZeroException>(() =>
calculator.Divide(10, 0));
}
```

Test Categories

Group tests into categories for easier execution.

csharp

```csharp
[Test, Category("Arithmetic")]
public void Multiply_ShouldReturnProduct()
{
    var calculator = new Calculator();
    int result = calculator.Multiply(3, 4);
    Assert.AreEqual(12, result);
}
```

Automated Testing Tools

Test automation speeds up validation in large projects, ensuring that code changes do not break existing features.

Integration Tests

Integration tests verify that different parts of the system work together.

csharp

```csharp
[TestFixture]
public class DatabaseTests
{
    private Database _db;

    [SetUp]
    public void Setup()
    {
        _db = new Database();
        _db.Connect("TestConnectionString");
    }

    [TearDown]
    public void Cleanup()
    {
        _db.Disconnect();
    }

    [Test]
    public void Query_ShouldReturnResults_WhenDataExists()
```

```
{
    var results = _db.Query("SELECT * FROM Users");
    Assert.IsNotEmpty(results);
}
}
```

Regression Tests

Regression tests ensure that new code changes do not introduce bugs into already existing features.

Continuous Execution with CI/CD

Tools such as Azure DevOps, GitHub Actions, and Jenkins allow you to integrate automated tests into CI/CD pipelines. Set up tasks to run tests whenever new changes are pushed to the repository.

Code Coverage Reports

Code coverage measures the proportion of code executed during tests. Tools like Coverlet can be used to generate detailed reports.

bash

```
dotnet test --collect:"XPlat Code Coverage"
```

Mocking

Mocking simulates external dependencies such as services or databases, allowing isolated unit testing.

csharp

```
using Moq;
```

```
[Test]
public void SendEmail_ShouldCallEmailService()
{
    var emailServiceMock = new Mock<IEmailService>();
    var notification = new
Notification(emailServiceMock.Object);

    notification.SendEmail("test@example.com", "Hello!");

    emailServiceMock.Verify(service =>
service.Send(It.IsAny<string>(), It.IsAny<string>()),
Times.Once);
}
```

Essential Practices in Testing and Debugging

- Write tests before implementing features: Adopt test-driven development (TDD).

- Prioritize automated tests: They are faster and more reliable than manual testing.

- Invest in detailed logs: Make it easier to identify problems by logging important information.

- Test in different scenarios: Include edge cases for robustness.

- Reproduce known bugs: Always create a test that

reproduces the bug before fixing it.

Common Error Resolution

Error: Breakpoint is not hit during execution.
Solution: Make sure the project is running in Debug mode and the compiled code matches the current file version.

Error: NUnit tests not detected in Visual Studio.
Solution: Check if the NUnit and NUnit3TestAdapter packages are installed and the project is set as a Test Project.

Error: Failure in interdependent tests.
Solution: Use [SetUp] and [TearDown] methods to ensure each test runs in a clean, independent environment.

Best Practices

- Use conditional breakpoints to reduce debugging time and focus on specific cases.

- Write small, isolated tests, avoiding direct external dependencies.

- Automate test execution in CI/CD pipelines to validate every new code change.

- Monitor coverage metrics to ensure critical areas are tested.

Strategic Summary

Structured testing and debugging ensure stability and predictability in C# development. Using tools such as Visual Studio, NUnit, and Moq allows rapid identification of failures and automated validation of features. By integrating these techniques into CI/CD flows and maintaining consistent code coverage, developers establish solid foundations for reliable deliveries, making maintenance, evolution, and scaling of professional systems easier.

CHAPTER 20. OPTIMIZATION AND PERFORMANCE

The performance of an application is one of the most important factors in the user experience. Optimized code ensures fast execution, efficient use of resources, and the scalability needed to handle high-demand scenarios. This chapter covers code optimization strategies, techniques for measuring and improving performance, and practices to reduce memory usage in C# applications.

Code Optimization Strategies

Understanding Performance

The optimization process begins by identifying bottlenecks —parts of the code or architecture that negatively impact efficiency. Before optimizing, it is essential to measure performance to avoid unnecessary changes.

Choosing the Right Data Structures

Selecting the right data structures can significantly improve performance. Choose structures based on expected usage.

- Use List<T> for dynamic lists and frequent index access.

- Use Dictionary<TKey, TValue> for fast key lookups.

- Use HashSet<T> to efficiently prevent duplicates.

csharp

```csharp
Dictionary<string, int> wordCounts = new Dictionary<string, int>();
wordCounts["example"] = 1; // Fast insertion
int count = wordCounts["example"]; // Efficient lookup
```

Reducing Algorithmic Complexity

Optimize algorithms to reduce complexity. Always prefer linear solutions ($O(n)$) over quadratic ones ($O(n^2)$) when possible.

csharp

```csharp
// O(n^2) complexity
for (int i = 0; i < list.Count; i++)
{
    for (int j = i + 1; j < list.Count; j++)
    {
        if (list[i] == list[j])
        {
            // Duplicate found
        }
    }
}
```

```csharp
// Optimized solution with HashSet - O(n)
HashSet<int> seen = new HashSet<int>();
foreach (var item in list)
{
    if (!seen.Add(item))
    {
        // Duplicate found
    }
}
```

Parallelism and Concurrency

To leverage multicore processors, distribute tasks that can be executed simultaneously.

csharp

```csharp
Parallel.For(0, 10, i =>
{
    Console.WriteLine($"Processing {i} on thread {Thread.CurrentThread.ManagedThreadId}");
});
```

Use Task for asynchronous operations and Parallel.For for parallel loops.

Result Caching

Store expensive computation results for reuse.

csharp

```csharp
Dictionary<int, int> cache = new Dictionary<int, int>();

int Fibonacci(int n)
{
    if (n <= 1) return n;

    if (cache.ContainsKey(n)) return cache[n];

    int result = Fibonacci(n - 1) + Fibonacci(n - 2);
    cache[n] = result;

    return result;
}
```

Avoiding Unnecessary Operations

Minimize redundant calculations inside loops.

csharp

```csharp
// Inefficient
for (int i = 0; i < list.Count; i++)
{
    if (list.Count > 0) // Evaluated every iteration
    {
        Console.WriteLine(list[i]);
    }
```

```
}
```

```
// Efficient
int count = list.Count;
for (int i = 0; i < count; i++)
{
    Console.WriteLine(list[i]);
}
```

Performance Measurement and Improvement

Profiler Tools

Tools like dotTrace, Visual Studio Profiler, and PerfView help identify bottlenecks. They provide detailed metrics such as time spent in methods and memory usage.

Measuring with Stopwatch

The Stopwatch class is a simple way to measure method execution time.

csharp

```
using System.Diagnostics;


Stopwatch stopwatch = Stopwatch.StartNew();


HeavyComputation();
```

```csharp
stopwatch.Stop();

Console.WriteLine($"Execution Time:
{stopwatch.ElapsedMilliseconds} ms");
```

Benchmarking

Use the BenchmarkDotNet library for precise performance measurement.

csharp

```csharp
using BenchmarkDotNet.Attributes;
using BenchmarkDotNet.Running;


public class MyBenchmark
{
    private List<int> numbers;

    [GlobalSetup]
    public void Setup()
    {
        numbers = Enumerable.Range(1, 10000).ToList();
    }

    [Benchmark]
    public void TestForLoop()
    {
```

```csharp
    for (int i = 0; i < numbers.Count; i++)
    {
        int x = numbers[i];
    }
}


[Benchmark]
public void TestForeachLoop()
{
    foreach (var number in numbers)
    {
        int x = number;
    }
}
}


BenchmarkRunner.Run<MyBenchmark>();
```

Load Testing

Use tools like Apache JMeter or K6 to simulate real-world load scenarios and assess application behavior under high demand.

Reducing Memory Usage

Object Management

Create objects only when needed and reuse instances whenever possible.

csharp

```
// Reusing StringBuilder to reduce allocations
StringBuilder builder = new StringBuilder();

for (int i = 0; i < 1000; i++)
{
    builder.Append(i.ToString());
}

string result = builder.ToString();
```

Avoid Large Objects on the Heap

Large objects are allocated on the Large Object Heap (LOH), which can cause memory fragmentation. Use smaller buffers to avoid the LOH.

csharp

```
byte[] buffer = new byte[85000]; // May go to the LOH
```

Resource Management

Implement the IDisposable interface to ensure unmanaged resources are released.

csharp

```
public class FileProcessor : IDisposable
```

```csharp
{
    private FileStream fileStream;

    public FileProcessor(string filePath)
    {
        fileStream = new FileStream(filePath, FileMode.Open);
    }

    public void Dispose()
    {
        fileStream?.Dispose();
    }
}
```

Avoid Memory Leaks

References held in static objects can prevent the garbage collector from freeing memory.

csharp

```csharp
public class MemoryLeak
{
    private static List<string> staticList = new List<string>();

    public void AddToStaticList(string item)
    {
        staticList.Add(item); // Keeps the reference alive
```

```
    }
}
```

Use Structs

In high-performance scenarios, prefer struct over class to avoid heap allocations.

csharp

```
public struct Point
{
    public int X { get; set; }
    public int Y { get; set; }
}
```

Object Pooling

Use object pools to reduce the cost of creating and destroying instances.

csharp

```
using System.Buffers;


ArrayPool<int> pool = ArrayPool<int>.Shared;


int[] rentedArray = pool.Rent(100);


// Perform operations on the array...
```

```
pool.Return(rentedArray);
```

Common Error Resolution

Error: Program consumes excessive memory during prolonged executions.
Solution: Check for objects held in memory by static references and implement IDisposable to release unmanaged resources.

Error: Poor performance in nested loops.
Solution: Reduce complexity using collections like HashSet or Dictionary and avoid repetitive calculations inside loops.

Error: Slow execution in parallel operations.
Solution: Avoid contention on shared resources and use thread-safe structures like ConcurrentDictionary when multiple threads access the same data.

Best Practices

- Use Stopwatch and profiling tools before applying optimizations.

- Prefer data structures suitable for the operation type (e.g., Dictionary for lookup, List for iteration).

- Reuse heavy object instances and use object pooling in high-frequency scenarios.

- Apply the principle of optimizing only what is proven to be a bottleneck.

Strategic Summary

Optimization in C# requires a balance between efficiency and clarity. Measuring, analyzing, and acting on specific bottlenecks results in real performance gains without compromising readability. With techniques such as rational memory usage, controlled parallelism, and appropriate structure selection, it is possible to build fast, stable, and scalable systems, ready to handle large data volumes and high execution loads.

CHAPTER 21. WORKING WITH EXTERNAL APIS

APIs (Application Programming Interfaces) are the backbone of communication between modern systems, allowing applications to interact with external services, databases, third-party platforms, and much more. In this chapter, we cover integration with REST and SOAP APIs, authentication and authorization with OAuth, and consuming real-time services.

Integration with REST and SOAP APIs

REST APIs

REST (Representational State Transfer) APIs are widely used due to their simplicity and scalability. They operate based on HTTP requests and use verbs like GET, POST, PUT, and DELETE to define operations.

Consuming a REST API

In C#, the HttpClient class is used to send HTTP requests and consume REST APIs.

csharp

```
using System.Net.Http;
```

```csharp
using System.Threading.Tasks;

public async Task FetchDataFromApi()
{
    using HttpClient client = new HttpClient();
    string url = "https://api.example.com/data";

    HttpResponseMessage response = await client.GetAsync(url);
    if (response.IsSuccessStatusCode)
    {
        string content = await
response.Content.ReadAsStringAsync();
        Console.WriteLine(content);
    }
    else
    {
        Console.WriteLine($"Error: {response.StatusCode}");
    }
}
```

Sending Data to an API

To send data, use the PostAsync method, specifying the request body as a StringContent.

csharp

```csharp
using System.Net.Http;
```

```csharp
using System.Text;
using System.Threading.Tasks;

public async Task PostDataToApi()
{
    using HttpClient client = new HttpClient();
    string url = "https://api.example.com/data";
    string json = "{\"name\":\"John Doe\",\"email\":
\"john@example.com\"}";

    HttpContent content = new StringContent(json,
Encoding.UTF8, "application/json");
    HttpResponseMessage response = await client.PostAsync(url,
content);

    if (response.IsSuccessStatusCode)
    {
        Console.WriteLine("Data sent successfully.");
    }
    else
    {
        Console.WriteLine($"Error: {response.StatusCode}");
    }
}
```

Handling Headers

Include custom headers such as authentication tokens using the DefaultRequestHeaders property.

csharp

```
client.DefaultRequestHeaders.Authorization =

    new
System.Net.Http.Headers.AuthenticationHeaderValue("Bearer",
"your_token");
```

SOAP APIs

SOAP (Simple Object Access Protocol) APIs use XML for information exchange and are common in legacy and enterprise systems.

Consuming a SOAP API

To consume SOAP APIs, use the HttpClient class or add service references in Visual Studio.

csharp

```
string soapEnvelope = @"<soap:Envelope xmlns:soap=""http://
schemas.xmlsoap.org/soap/envelope/"">

    <soap:Body>

        <GetInfo xmlns=""http://example.com/"">

            <Id>123</Id>

        </GetInfo>

    </soap:Body>

</soap:Envelope>";
```

```csharp
HttpContent content = new StringContent(soapEnvelope, Encoding.UTF8, "text/xml");
```

```csharp
using HttpClient client = new HttpClient();
client.DefaultRequestHeaders.Add("SOAPAction", "http://example.com/GetInfo");
```

```csharp
HttpResponseMessage response = await client.PostAsync("https://api.example.com/soap", content);
string responseContent = await response.Content.ReadAsStringAsync();
Console.WriteLine(responseContent);
```

Adding Service References

In Visual Studio:

1. Go to Add Service in the project menu.

2. Enter the WSDL URL of the SOAP API.

3. Use the generated classes to make calls.

csharp

```csharp
ServiceReference.Client client = new ServiceReference.Client();
var response = client.GetInfo(123);
Console.WriteLine(response);
```

Authentication and Authorization with OAuth

OAuth is a standard protocol for secure authentication, allowing users to authorize applications to access resources without sharing their credentials.

OAuth 2.0 Authentication Flow

1. **User Authorization:** The user grants permission to the client.

2. **Obtaining the Access Token:** The client requests an access token from the server.

3. **Accessing the Resource:** The client uses the token to access the protected API.

Obtaining a Token

Tokens are obtained by sending information to the OAuth server, usually with HttpClient.

csharp

```csharp
using System.Net.Http;
using System.Collections.Generic;
using System.Threading.Tasks;

public async Task<string> GetOAuthToken()
{
    using HttpClient client = new HttpClient();
    string tokenUrl = "https://auth.example.com/token";
```

```csharp
    var requestData = new Dictionary<string, string>
    {
        { "grant_type", "client_credentials" },
        { "client_id", "your_client_id" },
        { "client_secret", "your_client_secret" }
    };


    HttpResponseMessage response =
await client.PostAsync(tokenUrl, new
FormUrlEncodedContent(requestData));
    if (response.IsSuccessStatusCode)
    {
        string jsonResponse = await
response.Content.ReadAsStringAsync();
        var token =
Newtonsoft.Json.JsonConvert.DeserializeObject<dynamic>(jso
nResponse);
        return token.access_token;
    }


    throw new Exception("Failed to retrieve token.");
}
```

Using the Token

Include the token in the authorization headers.

csharp

```
client.DefaultRequestHeaders.Authorization =

    new
System.Net.Http.Headers.AuthenticationHeaderValue("Bearer",
token);
```

Automatic Token Renewal

Access tokens are short-lived. Store the refresh token to renew expired tokens.

csharp

```
var requestData = new Dictionary<string, string>

{

    { "grant_type", "refresh_token" },

    { "refresh_token", "your_refresh_token" },

    { "client_id", "your_client_id" },

    { "client_secret", "your_client_secret" }

};
```

Consuming Real-Time Services

WebSocket-Based APIs

WebSockets provide real-time, bidirectional communication, ideal for chat apps, monitoring systems, and live updates.

Establishing a WebSocket Connection:

csharp

```
using System.Net.WebSockets;
```

```csharp
using System.Text;
using System.Threading;


public async Task ConnectWebSocket()
{
    using ClientWebSocket socket = new ClientWebSocket();
    await socket.ConnectAsync(new Uri("wss://example.com/socket"), CancellationToken.None);


    byte[] buffer = new byte[1024];
    var segment = new ArraySegment<byte>(buffer);


    WebSocketReceiveResult result = await socket.ReceiveAsync(segment, CancellationToken.None);
    string message = Encoding.UTF8.GetString(buffer, 0, result.Count);
    Console.WriteLine($"Received: {message}");
}
```

Use the SendAsync method to send messages:

csharp

```csharp
string message = "Hello WebSocket!";
byte[] buffer = Encoding.UTF8.GetBytes(message);


await socket.SendAsync(new ArraySegment<byte>(buffer), WebSocketMessageType.Text, true, CancellationToken.None);
```

Server-Sent Events (SSE) APIs

SSE provides continuous updates from the server to the client.

csharp

```csharp
using System.Net.Http;

public async Task ReceiveServerSentEvents()
{
    using HttpClient client = new HttpClient();
    var response = await client.GetStreamAsync("https://example.com/sse");

    using var reader = new StreamReader(response);
    while (!reader.EndOfStream)
    {
        string eventData = await reader.ReadLineAsync();
        Console.WriteLine(eventData);
    }
}
```

Essential Practices When Working with External APIs

- **Data Validation:** Always validate data received from external APIs before use.

- **Error Handling:** Implement strategies to handle connection failures and invalid responses.

- **Rate Limiting:** Respect the API's usage policies to avoid being blocked.

- **Response Caching:** For infrequently changing data, implement a cache to reduce repetitive calls.

- **Documentation:** Read the API documentation to understand limits, available methods, and required parameters.

Common Error Resolution

Error: Failed to consume REST endpoint (status 401 or 403).
Solution: Check if the OAuth token is valid and is sent in the Authorization header in the correct format.

Error: Failed to consume SOAP API.
Solution: Confirm that the XML envelope matches the WSDL standard and the SOAPAction header is set properly.

Error: HTTP call timeout.
Solution: Adjust HttpClient.Timeout and implement retry logic for transient failures.

Best Practices

- Reuse HttpClient instances to avoid socket exhaustion.

- Validate and sanitize all data received from external APIs before processing.

- Use caching to reduce redundant calls and optimize performance.

Strategic Summary

Integration with external APIs in C# connects applications to

REST and SOAP services, extending their functionality. With proper use of HttpClient, OAuth authentication, and structured response handling, it's possible to consume data securely and efficiently. Adopting simple practices like connection reuse, input validation, and result caching ensures stable, fast, and scalable communications between systems.

CHAPTER 22. C# FOR IOT AND DEVICES

The Internet of Things (IoT) connects physical devices to the internet, enabling communication and remote control. C#, together with the .NET platform, provides a solid foundation for programming IoT solutions due to its versatility, hardware support, and integration capabilities with servers. In this module, we will detail how to program IoT devices with .NET, establish communication between devices and servers, and implement practical automations.

Programming IoT Devices with .NET
IoT Fundamentals

IoT devices consist of sensors, actuators, and processors that collect, transmit, and execute data. .NET, especially with the support of .NET IoT Libraries, simplifies embedded device programming and communication with peripherals.

Setting up the Environment:

To get started, install the .NET SDK and add specific libraries for IoT. Use a device such as a Raspberry Pi to implement embedded applications.

1. Setting Up the Environment on Raspberry Pi:
- Install the .NET Runtime on the device.

- Set up remote access via SSH for direct development.

2. Install Libraries: Install NuGet packages like

> System.Device.Gpio and Iot.Device.Bindings to interact with hardware.

bash

```
dotnet add package System.Device.Gpio
dotnet add package Iot.Device.Bindings
```

Controlling GPIO with C#

GPIO (General Purpose Input/Output) pins allow direct interactions with sensors and actuators.

Configuring GPIO:

Use the System.Device.Gpio library to control GPIO pins.

csharp

```csharp
using System.Device.Gpio;

public class GpioControllerExample
{
    public void ControlLed()
    {
        int ledPin = 18; // GPIO pin number
        GpioController controller = new GpioController();

        controller.OpenPin(ledPin, PinMode.Output);

        controller.Write(ledPin, PinValue.High); // Turns on the LED
```

```
    Thread.Sleep(1000);              // Waits 1 second
    controller.Write(ledPin, PinValue.Low); // Turns off the
LED

    controller.ClosePin(ledPin);
  }
}
```

This example triggers an LED connected to pin 18, turning it on and off with a one-second interval.

Reading Sensor Data

IoT devices often use sensors to collect data. Use GPIO for reading input values.

csharp

```
public void ReadSensor()
{
    int sensorPin = 17;
    GpioController controller = new GpioController();

    controller.OpenPin(sensorPin, PinMode.Input);

    PinValue value = controller.Read(sensorPin);
    Console.WriteLine($"Sensor Value: {value}");
```

```csharp
controller.ClosePin(sensorPin);
}
```

Communication Protocols with Peripherals

I2C (Inter-Integrated Circuit)

I2C is a widely used protocol for communicating with sensors and other devices.

csharp

```csharp
using System.Device.I2c;


public void ReadI2cDevice()
{
    var settings = new I2cConnectionSettings(1, 0x40); // Device address
    using var device = I2cDevice.Create(settings);


    Span<byte> buffer = stackalloc byte[2];
    device.Read(buffer);


    Console.WriteLine($"Data: {buffer[0]}, {buffer[1]}");
}
```

SPI (Serial Peripheral Interface)

SPI is another common protocol for fast communication between devices.

csharp

```
using System.Device.Spi;


public void ReadSpiDevice()
{
    var settings = new SpiConnectionSettings(0, 0); // Bus 0, Chip Select 0
    using var device = SpiDevice.Create(settings);

    Span<byte> buffer = stackalloc byte[2];
    device.Read(buffer);

    Console.WriteLine($"Data: {buffer[0]}, {buffer[1]}");
}
```

Communication between Devices and Servers

IoT devices often send data to servers or receive it for remote control. .NET makes this communication easy with REST APIs, MQTT, and WebSockets.

Sending Data with REST APIs

Data can be sent to a server using HttpClient.

csharp

```
using System.Net.Http;
```

```csharp
using System.Text.Json;
using System.Threading.Tasks;

public async Task SendDataToServer(double temperature)
{
    using HttpClient client = new HttpClient();
    string url = "https://server.example.com/api/temperature";

    var data = new { DeviceId = "Sensor1", Temperature = temperature };
    string json = JsonSerializer.Serialize(data);

    HttpContent content = new StringContent(json, Encoding.UTF8, "application/json");
    await client.PostAsync(url, content);
}
```

MQTT Communication

MQTT (Message Queuing Telemetry Transport) is ideal for IoT systems due to its efficiency and bidirectional communication support.

csharp

```csharp
using MQTTnet;
using MQTTnet.Client;
using MQTTnet.Client.Options;
using System.Text;
```

```
using System.Threading.Tasks;

public async Task ConnectToMqtt()
{
    var factory = new MqttFactory();
    using var client = factory.CreateMqttClient();

    var options = new MqttClientOptionsBuilder()
        .WithClientId("Device1")
        .WithTcpServer("mqtt.example.com", 1883)
        .Build();

    client.UseConnectedHandler(e =>
Console.WriteLine("Connected to MQTT broker."));
    client.UseApplicationMessageReceivedHandler(e =>
        Console.WriteLine($"Received:
{Encoding.UTF8.GetString(e.ApplicationMessage.Payload)}"));

    await client.ConnectAsync(options);

    await client.PublishAsync("sensor/data",
Encoding.UTF8.GetBytes("Temperature: 22.5"));
}
```

Using WebSockets

WebSockets enable real-time communication with servers.

csharp

```csharp
using System.Net.WebSockets;

using System.Text;

using System.Threading;


public async Task ConnectWebSocket()

{

    using var socket = new ClientWebSocket();

    await socket.ConnectAsync(new Uri("wss://
server.example.com"), CancellationToken.None);


    byte[] message = Encoding.UTF8.GetBytes("Hello from IoT
device");

    await socket.SendAsync(new
ArraySegment<byte>(message), WebSocketMessageType.Text,
true, CancellationToken.None);

}
```

Practical Automation Examples

Lighting Automation

Create a system that turns lights on or off based on a light sensor reading.

csharp

```csharp
public void AutomateLighting()

{
```

```
int lightPin = 22;
int sensorPin = 23;
GpioController controller = new GpioController();


controller.OpenPin(lightPin, PinMode.Output);
controller.OpenPin(sensorPin, PinMode.Input);


while (true)
{
    PinValue sensorValue = controller.Read(sensorPin);
    if (sensorValue == PinValue.Low)
    {
        controller.Write(lightPin, PinValue.High); // Turns on
the light
    }
    else
    {
        controller.Write(lightPin, PinValue.Low); // Turns off
the light
    }
    Thread.Sleep(500);
  }
}
```

Remote Temperature Monitoring

Combine temperature sensors with MQTT communication for remote environment monitoring.

csharp

```
public async Task MonitorTemperature()
{
    double temperature = GetTemperatureFromSensor(); // Function to read the sensor

    await ConnectToMqtt();
    await PublishTemperature(temperature);
}


private double GetTemperatureFromSensor()
{
    // Simulate reading from the sensor
    return 25.3;
}


private async Task PublishTemperature(double temperature)
{
    var factory = new MqttFactory();
    using var client = factory.CreateMqttClient();

    var options = new MqttClientOptionsBuilder()
        .WithClientId("TemperatureSensor")
```

```
    .WithTcpServer("mqtt.example.com", 1883)
    .Build();

await client.ConnectAsync(options);

string payload = $"{{ \"temperature\": {temperature} }}";
await client.PublishAsync("home/temperature",
Encoding.UTF8.GetBytes(payload));
}
```

Device Control via Application

Integrate an IoT device with a web or mobile application for remote control.

csharp

```
public void ControlDevice(string command)
{
    int devicePin = 21;
    GpioController controller = new GpioController();
    controller.OpenPin(devicePin, PinMode.Output);

    if (command == "ON")
    {
        controller.Write(devicePin, PinValue.High);
    }
    else if (command == "OFF")
```

```
{
    controller.Write(devicePin, PinValue.Low);
}
}
```

Common Error Resolution

Error: GPIO does not respond to commands.
Solution: Check if the pin number matches the device's physical mapping and whether hardware access permissions are correct.

Error: MQTT connection failure.
Solution: Confirm the broker address, the port used, and authentication credentials, and ensure the firewall allows connections on port 1883.

Error: Sensor communication returns incorrect values.
Solution: Review the protocol configuration (I2C or SPI), the device address, and the physical wiring.

Best Practices

- Use official .NET IoT libraries to ensure hardware compatibility.

- Implement automatic reconnection in protocols such as MQTT and WebSockets.

- Avoid infinite loops without delay — use Thread.Sleep() or timers to reduce power consumption.

Strategic Summary

C# and .NET provide a complete ecosystem for IoT device control and monitoring. Support for GPIO, I2C, SPI, REST, MQTT, and WebSockets allows easy and stable integration of sensors, actuators, and servers. With best practices for reconnection, validation, and energy efficiency, developers can create secure, scalable, and automation-ready IoT solutions for large-scale deployment.

CAPÍTULO 23. REAL PROJECTS WITH C#

Working on real projects is essential to consolidate learning and apply theoretical concepts in practice. This chapter presents three example projects in C#, covering the development of a task management application, the creation of a secure API, and the implementation of an inventory system. Each model uses modern practices and follows widely adopted industry standards.

1.   Developing a Task Management Application

A task management application allows users to organize activities, set priorities, and track progress. Let's build an application based on the MVC pattern with ASP.NET Core.

Initial Setup

Create the Project:

- Open Visual Studio.
- Select ASP.NET Core Web Application (MVC Template).
- Configure the project as "TaskManager".

Add Required Packages:

Add Entity Framework Core for database handling.

bash

```
dotnet add package Microsoft.EntityFrameworkCore

dotnet add package Microsoft.EntityFrameworkCore.SqlServer
```

Project Structure

- **Model:** Represents the task entity.
- **Controller:** Contains the logic for data handling and navigation.
- **View:** Defines the user interface.

Creating the Model

Create the TaskItem class in the Models directory.

csharp

```csharp
public class TaskItem
{
    public int Id { get; set; }
    public string Title { get; set; }
    public string Description { get; set; }
    public bool IsCompleted { get; set; }
    public DateTime CreatedAt { get; set; } = DateTime.Now;
}
```

Configuring the Database

Add the ApplicationDbContext class to manage the connection with the database.

csharp

```csharp
using Microsoft.EntityFrameworkCore;


public class ApplicationDbContext : DbContext
```

```csharp
{
    public DbSet<TaskItem> Tasks { get; set; }

    protected override void
OnConfiguring(DbContextOptionsBuilder options)
    {
        options.UseSqlServer("YourConnectionString");
    }
}
```

Run migrations to create the table in the database:

bash

```bash
dotnet ef migrations add InitialCreate
dotnet ef database update
```

Creating the Controller

Add a controller to manage the tasks.

csharp

```csharp
using Microsoft.AspNetCore.Mvc;
using System.Linq;

public class TasksController : Controller
{
    private readonly ApplicationDbContext _context;
```

```
public TasksController(ApplicationDbContext context)
{
    _context = context;
}

public IActionResult Index()
{
    var tasks = _context.Tasks.ToList();
    return View(tasks);
}

public IActionResult Create() => View();

[HttpPost]
public IActionResult Create(TaskItem task)
{
    _context.Tasks.Add(task);
    _context.SaveChanges();
    return RedirectToAction("Index");
}
}
```

Creating the Views

Implement the interface to list and create tasks. In the Views/

Tasks directory, add Index.cshtml and Create.cshtml.

Index.cshtml:

html

```
@model IEnumerable<TaskItem>


<h2>Task List</h2>
<table>
    <thead>
        <tr>
            <th>Title</th>
            <th>Description</th>
            <th>Status</th>
            <th>Actions</th>
        </tr>
    </thead>
    <tbody>
        @foreach (var task in Model)
        {
            <tr>
                <td>@task.Title</td>
                <td>@task.Description</td>
                <td>@(task.IsCompleted ? "Completed" :
"Pending")</td>
                <td>
                    <a href="/Tasks/Edit/@task.Id">Edit</a>
                    <a href="/Tasks/Delete/@task.Id">Delete</a>
```

```
            </td>
        </tr>
    }
    </tbody>
</table>
```

Create.cshtml:

html

```
@model TaskItem

<h2>Create Task</h2>
<form asp-action="Create" method="post">
    <label>Title:</label>
    <input asp-for="Title" />
    <br />
    <label>Description:</label>
    <textarea asp-for="Description"></textarea>
    <br />
    <button type="submit">Save</button>
</form>
```

2. Creating a Complete API with Integrated Security

APIs are essential for modern applications. Let's develop a RESTful API to manage users with JWT authentication.

Initial Setup

- Create the Project: In Visual Studio, create an ASP.NET Core API project called "UserApi".

Add Required Packages:

bash

```
dotnet add package Microsoft.EntityFrameworkCore

dotnet add package Microsoft.EntityFrameworkCore.SqlServer

dotnet add package
Microsoft.AspNetCore.Authentication.JwtBearer
```

Project Structure

Configuring the Model

Add the User class in the Models directory.

csharp

```
public class User
{
    public int Id { get; set; }
    public string Username { get; set; }
    public string Password { get; set; }
}
```

Configuring the Context

Add ApplicationDbContext.

csharp

```
using Microsoft.EntityFrameworkCore;
```

```csharp
public class ApplicationDbContext : DbContext
{
    public DbSet<User> Users { get; set; }

    protected override void
OnConfiguring(DbContextOptionsBuilder options)
    {
        options.UseSqlServer("YourConnectionString");
    }
}
```

Adding JWT Authentication

Configure JWT in Program.cs.

csharp

```csharp
builder.Services.AddAuthentication("Bearer")
    .AddJwtBearer(options =>
    {
        options.TokenValidationParameters = new
TokenValidationParameters
        {
            ValidateIssuer = true,
            ValidateAudience = true,
            ValidateLifetime = true,
            ValidateIssuerSigningKey = true,
```

```
        ValidIssuer = "your_issuer",

        ValidAudience = "your_audience",

        IssuerSigningKey = new
SymmetricSecurityKey(Encoding.UTF8.GetBytes("your_secret_
key"))
    };
});
```

Creating Controllers

Add a controller for authentication.

csharp

```
[ApiController]

[Route("api/[controller]")]

public class AuthController : ControllerBase

{

    private readonly ApplicationDbContext _context;

    public AuthController(ApplicationDbContext context)

    {

        _context = context;

    }

    [HttpPost("login")]

    public IActionResult Login([FromBody] User user)

    {
```

```csharp
    var dbUser = _context.Users.FirstOrDefault(u =>
u.Username == user.Username);

    if (dbUser == null || dbUser.Password != user.Password)
    {
        return Unauthorized();
    }

    var token = GenerateJwtToken();
    return Ok(new { token });
}


private string GenerateJwtToken()
{
    var securityKey = new
SymmetricSecurityKey(Encoding.UTF8.GetBytes("your_secret_
key"));
    var credentials = new SigningCredentials(securityKey,
SecurityAlgorithms.HmacSha256);

    var token = new JwtSecurityToken(
        issuer: "your_issuer",
        audience: "your_audience",
        expires: DateTime.Now.AddHours(1),
        signingCredentials: credentials);

    return new
```

```csharp
JwtSecurityTokenHandler().WriteToken(token);
    }
}
```

3. Inventory System Project

This project manages stock items, with functionalities to add, remove, and list products.

Setup

Create an ASP.NET Core MVC project and configure the entity and database structure for products.

Model:

csharp

```csharp
public class Product
{
    public int Id { get; set; }
    public string Name { get; set; }
    public int Quantity { get; set; }
    public decimal Price { get; set; }
}
```

Controller:

csharp

```csharp
public class InventoryController : Controller
{
    private readonly ApplicationDbContext _context;
```

```csharp
public InventoryController(ApplicationDbContext context)
{
    _context = context;
}

public IActionResult Index()
{
    var products = _context.Products.ToList();
    return View(products);
}

[HttpPost]
public IActionResult Add(Product product)
{
    _context.Products.Add(product);
    _context.SaveChanges();
    return RedirectToAction("Index");
}
}
```

View:

html

```
@model IEnumerable<Product>
```

```
<h2>Inventory</h2>
<table>
   <thead>
     <tr>
       <th>Name</th>
       <th>Quantity</th>
       <th>Price</th>
     </tr>
   </thead>
   <tbody>
     @foreach (var product in Model)
     {
       <tr>
         <td>@product.Name</td>
         <td>@product.Quantity</td>
         <td>@product.Price</td>
       </tr>
     }
   </tbody>
</table>
```

Common Error Resolution

Error: Failure to connect to the database in projects.
Solution: Check the connection string, the active SQL server, and if the migrations were properly applied with dotnet ef database

update.

Error: Invalid or expired JWT token.
Solution: Adjust the expiration time and confirm that issuer, audience, and secret key match between the token generator and validator.

Error: Data does not appear in the views.
Solution: Confirm that the model is being correctly returned from the controller and that the @model at the top of the view matches the type sent.

Best Practices

- Separate business logic from the interface layer to keep code clean and testable.

- Use JWT authentication only via HTTPS and store tokens securely.

- Apply input validation to all forms before persisting data.

Strategic Summary

Real-world projects in C# consolidate fundamental concepts of professional development. Task management demonstrates the use of MVC with persistence via Entity Framework, the JWT API exemplifies secure authentication and access control, and the inventory system reinforces efficient data handling. These practical models form a solid foundation for creating new structured, secure, and scalable solutions, applying the resources of the .NET ecosystem in production scenarios.

CHAPTER 24. FUTURE TRENDS OF C#

The C# language has established itself as one of the most robust and versatile for software development. With its continuous evolution, driven by the .NET platform, C# continues to lead technological innovations and meet market demands in areas such as artificial intelligence (AI), Internet of Things (IoT), and cloud computing. This chapter discusses the future perspectives of C#, new features in .NET, and the language's impact on emerging areas.

Strategic Direction of C#

C# continues to evolve with a focus on productivity, performance, and simplicity. Each new version introduces features that eliminate complexity, enhance code readability, and optimize execution. The language maintains a balance between innovation and stability, ensuring accessibility for both beginners and experienced developers.

Key areas of evolution:

- Functional Programming: Increasing adoption of functional characteristics, such as records and more concise expressions.

- Concurrent and Parallel Programming: Advances in async/await and introduction of new APIs for more intuitive handling of concurrent tasks.

- Integration with AI: Features to facilitate the creation

and integration of machine learning models directly into the .NET ecosystem.

Cross-Platform Expansion

The introduction of .NET 6 and .NET 7 has solidified the vision of a truly cross-platform framework. The future of C# is tied to this goal, enabling the language to be used for development in:

- Web: Using ASP.NET Core.

- Desktop: Applications on Windows, Linux, and macOS with native support.

- Mobile: Integrated development with MAUI (Multi-platform App UI).

- Games: Unity remains one of the most popular engines for game development with C#.

Integration between platforms reduces development costs and expands the reach of applications built with C#.

New Features in .NET and Market Trends

New Features in .NET

The .NET ecosystem has expanded to support new market demands, with features designed for high performance and scalability.

Performance Improvements:

- Optimized APIs for data manipulation.

- Adoption of intermediate languages (such as Span<T>) to reduce memory usage.

Simplification of Development:

- Minimization of configuration files.

- Support for top-level programs, eliminating the need for class definitions for simple scripts.

Integration with Machine Learning:

- The ML.NET library facilitates building AI models directly in .NET, allowing developers to use machine learning algorithms with minimal initial setup.

Container Adoption:

- Enhanced tools for running and managing .NET applications in container environments, such as Docker and Kubernetes.

Market Trends

With the growing demand for digital solutions, the global market seeks languages that balance efficiency, security, and productivity. C# continues to be a popular choice for meeting needs across various areas.

Highlights:

- Cloud Development: Native integration with services like Azure and AWS.

- Industrial Automation: Extensive use in systems that connect machines and IoT devices.

- Real-Time Applications: With ASP.NET SignalR, C# is widely used for chatbots, online games, and monitoring systems.

Impact in Emerging Areas

Artificial Intelligence (AI)

Machine learning and artificial intelligence are transforming the way technological solutions are developed. C#, with its ML.NET library, enables developers to create machine learning models without the need for external languages like Python.

Creating a Simple AI Model with ML.NET

Below is an example of how to train a regression model to predict house prices.

Install the ML.NET package:

bash

```
dotnet add package Microsoft.ML
```

Configure the model:

csharp

```
using Microsoft.ML;
using Microsoft.ML.Data;

public class HouseData
{
    public float Size { get; set; }
    public float Price { get; set; }
}
```

```csharp
public class Prediction
{
    [ColumnName("Score")]
    public float PredictedPrice { get; set; }
}


var context = new MLContext();


var data = new List<HouseData>
{
    new HouseData { Size = 1.1F, Price = 1.2F },
    new HouseData { Size = 1.9F, Price = 2.3F },
    new HouseData { Size = 2.8F, Price = 3.0F }
};


var trainingData = context.Data.LoadFromEnumerable(data);


var pipeline = context.Transforms.Concatenate("Features",
new[] { "Size" })
    .Append(context.Regression.Trainers.Sdca());


var model = pipeline.Fit(trainingData);


var prediction = model.CreatePredictionEngine<HouseData,
```

```csharp
Prediction>(context)
    .Predict(new HouseData { Size = 2.5F });
```

```csharp
Console.WriteLine($"Predicted price:
{prediction.PredictedPrice}");
```

This example demonstrates how C# is ready to meet modern machine learning demands.

Internet of Things (IoT)

The exponential growth of connected devices creates opportunities for languages like C#, which offer simplified integration with hardware and communication protocols.

Temperature Monitoring with Sensors

C# and .NET IoT Libraries allow reading data from sensors, such as temperature monitoring.

csharp

```csharp
using System.Device.Gpio;


public void MonitorTemperature()
{
    int sensorPin = 18;
    GpioController controller = new GpioController();


    controller.OpenPin(sensorPin, PinMode.Input);
```

```csharp
while (true)
{
    var value = controller.Read(sensorPin);
    Console.WriteLine($"Temperature: {value}");
    Thread.Sleep(1000);
}
}
```

The ease of integration with sensors and devices makes C# a powerful tool for IoT systems.

Augmented and Virtual Reality

The development of augmented reality (AR) and virtual reality (VR) applications is on the rise. Unity, the main graphics engine used to create these experiences, uses C# as the primary language for behavior and interaction programming.

Implementing Simple Interactions

Below is a script that allows an object to respond to user clicks:

```csharp
csharp
using UnityEngine;

public class ObjectClick : MonoBehaviour
{
```

```
void OnMouseDown()
{
    Debug.Log("Object clicked!");
    GetComponent<Renderer>().material.color = Color.red;
}
}
```

With Unity and C#, you can create interactive worlds for games, simulations, and training.

The Continuous Evolution of C#

Microsoft continues to invest in the expansion of C# and .NET to meet new demands, with constant improvements in security, performance, and productivity.

- Adaptation to Quantum Computing: The Microsoft Q# project is already integrated with .NET, indicating openness to C#-based languages in quantum contexts.

- Support for Generative AI: The language is moving towards greater integration with generative AI, enabling workflow automation and smarter solutions.

Common Error Resolution

Error: Failure to execute ML.NET code.
Solution: Confirm the installation of the Microsoft.ML package, validate the input data format, and ensure the model is trained before prediction.

Error: GPIO does not respond in IoT projects.
Solution: Check hardware access permissions, the correct pin

number, and if the controller has been properly initialized.

Error: Exception in Unity scripts.
Solution: Confirm that the script is attached to an active GameObject and that the method is in the correct lifecycle (Start, Update, or OnMouseDown).

Best Practices

- Keep code compatible with current versions of .NET to ensure support and performance.

- Follow C# updates and gradually adopt new features like records, pattern matching, and async streams.

- Explore official libraries for AI, IoT, and Unity, avoiding unmaintained external dependencies.

Strategic Summary

C# is continuously advancing as a reference language for innovation and reliability. Its ecosystem integrates machine learning, IoT devices, and immersive experiences with Unity, maintaining a focus on performance and productivity. The convergence between .NET, AI, and multiplatforms ensures that C# remains at the center of technological transformation, ready for the next generations of intelligent and connected development.

CAPÍTULO 25. CAREER TIPS AND CERTIFICATIONS

Building a solid career in technology requires more than just technical skills: it takes planning, interview preparation, and certifications that validate your knowledge. This module covers strategies to stand out in technical interviews, the main certifications related to C# and .NET, and how to plan a promising career focused on this language.

Technical Interview Preparation

Understanding the Selection Process

Technology companies usually divide the selection process into stages:

- Initial Screening: Generally based on résumé and portfolio.

- Online Technical Tests: Assessment of programming knowledge.

- Technical Interviews: Include real-time problem solving.

- Behavioral Interviews: Evaluation of cultural alignment and interpersonal skills.

Technical Preparation

Review the Fundamentals

Master the basics of C# and algorithms. Focus on:

- Data structures: arrays, lists, dictionaries, trees, and graphs.

- Algorithms: sorting, searching, and optimization problems.

- Design patterns: Singleton, Factory, Observer.

Example of a sorting algorithm in C#:

csharp

```csharp
public void BubbleSort(int[] array)
{
    for (int i = 0; i < array.Length - 1; i++)
    {
        for (int j = 0; j < array.Length - i - 1; j++)
        {
            if (array[j] > array[j + 1])
            {
                int temp = array[j];
                array[j] = array[j + 1];
                array[j + 1] = temp;
            }
        }
    }
}
```

Practice Problems

Solve problems on platforms like HackerRank or LeetCode, prioritizing questions focused on:

- String manipulation.

- Operations on collections.

- Efficient memory management.

Practical challenge: reverse a string without using built-in methods.

csharp

```csharp
public string ReverseString(string input)
{
    char[] reversed = new char[input.Length];
    for (int i = 0, j = input.Length - 1; i < input.Length; i++, j--)
    {
        reversed[i] = input[j];
    }
    return new string(reversed);
}
```

Mock Interviews

Conduct mock interviews with colleagues or mentors. During the simulations:

- Explain your reasoning as you write the code.

- Focus on solving problems clearly and efficiently.

System Design Interview Preparation

Large companies may include system design interviews. Practice creating diagrams and software architecture.

Example: design a task management system.

- Divide the system into services: authentication, task API, database.

- Use diagrams to represent data and communication flows.

Behavioral Tips

Besides technical knowledge, companies assess communication skills and the ability to solve problems under pressure. Use the STAR methodology (Situation, Task, Action, Result) to structure answers to behavioral questions.

Main C# and .NET Certifications

Certifications help validate technical skills and increase professional credibility. They are especially useful for beginners or professionals looking to change careers.

Microsoft Certified: Azure Developer Associate

This certification is relevant for developers who use C# to build cloud applications with Azure.

Topics Covered:

- Development of APIs and functions in Azure.

- Integration with services like Azure Storage and Cosmos DB.

- Implementation of security and authentication.

Preparation:

- Study cloud computing concepts and Azure services.

- Practice developing APIs using ASP.NET Core.

Example of integration with Azure Blob Storage in C#:

csharp

```csharp
using Azure.Storage.Blobs;

public async Task UploadToBlobAsync(string connectionString, string containerName, string filePath)
{
    BlobServiceClient blobServiceClient = new BlobServiceClient(connectionString);
    BlobContainerClient containerClient = blobServiceClient.GetBlobContainerClient(containerName);

    string fileName = Path.GetFileName(filePath);
    BlobClient blobClient = containerClient.GetBlobClient(fileName);

    await blobClient.UploadAsync(filePath, true);
    Console.WriteLine($"File {fileName} uploaded successfully.");
}
```

Microsoft Certified: .NET Developer Specialist

This certification is ideal for validating specific skills in developing applications with C# and .NET.

Topics Covered:

- Web development with ASP.NET Core.

- API consumption and data manipulation.

- Code testing and debugging.

Preparation:

- Build practical projects to explore ASP.NET Core features, such as authentication and middleware.

- Practice unit testing with NUnit.

Example of custom middleware in ASP.NET Core:

csharp

```csharp
public class LoggingMiddleware
{
    private readonly RequestDelegate _next;

    public LoggingMiddleware(RequestDelegate next)
    {
        _next = next;
    }
```

```
public async Task InvokeAsync(HttpContext context)
{
    Console.WriteLine($"Request: {context.Request.Method} {context.Request.Path}");
    await _next(context);
}
}


// Add to the pipeline
app.UseMiddleware<LoggingMiddleware>();
```

Complementary Certifications

In addition to Microsoft certifications, the following can add value to your résumé:

- Certified Kubernetes Application Developer (CKAD): For developers using containers.

- AWS Certified Developer – Associate: For integration with AWS services.

- Certified Information Systems Security Professional (CISSP): For those working with application security.

Career Planning Focused on C#

Choosing a Direction

C# is a versatile language, and career planning can be shaped based on personal interests and goals. Some areas of focus include:

- Web Development: Focus on ASP.NET Core and RESTful APIs.

- Game Development: Use Unity to create 2D, 3D, and virtual reality games.

- Enterprise Systems: Integration of robust applications with databases and corporate services.

- Cloud: Development of scalable solutions in Azure and AWS.

- IoT and Automation: Programming of connected devices and sensors.

Building a Portfolio

Develop projects that demonstrate practical skills and include them in your portfolio. Examples:

- A simple task manager.

- A secure API integrated with JWT authentication.

- A basic game developed in Unity.

Example of a basic API in ASP.NET Core:

csharp

```csharp
[ApiController]
[Route("api/[controller]")]
public class ProductsController : ControllerBase
{
```

```csharp
    private static List<Product> products = new List<Product>
    {
        new Product { Id = 1, Name = "Laptop", Price = 1000 },
        new Product { Id = 2, Name = "Phone", Price = 500 }
    };


    [HttpGet]
    public IEnumerable<Product> GetProducts() => products;


    [HttpPost]
    public IActionResult AddProduct([FromBody] Product
product)
    {
        products.Add(product);
        return Ok(product);
    }
}


public class Product
{
    public int Id { get; set; }
    public string Name { get; set; }
    public decimal Price { get; set; }
}
```

Networking and Online Presence

- Participation in Events: Attend hackathons, conferences, and meetups related to C# and .NET.

- Contribution to Open Source: Contribute to projects on GitHub.

- LinkedIn and Online Portfolios: Keep your profile updated and share relevant projects.

Setting Long-Term Goals

Define clear objectives:

- Short term: Complete a certification or build a robust portfolio.

- Medium term: Become a specialist in a specific area, such as IoT or web development.

- Long term: Take on leadership roles, such as software architect or engineering manager.

Common Error Resolution

Error: Lack of practical projects in your portfolio.
Solution: Build real applications focusing on market problems — APIs, dashboards, or integrations — and publish on GitHub with documentation.

Error: Difficulty in technical interviews.
Solution: Practice solving algorithms on platforms like HackerRank and LeetCode, explaining your reasoning out loud.

Error: Certification failed due to lack of focus on content.
Solution: Study with official Microsoft guides and practice labs with Azure and .NET before taking the exam.

Best Practices

- Plan your learning path and set short- and long-term goals.

- Prioritize certifications directly related to your desired area of expertise.

- Maintain an active presence on LinkedIn and GitHub to demonstrate technical growth.

Strategic Summary

Success in a C# career requires more than technical mastery — it requires strategy, certifications, and professional visibility. With interview preparation, certifications like Azure Developer and .NET Specialist, and a solid portfolio, the developer is positioned competitively in the global market. The combination of continuous learning, networking, and constant practice is the most effective path to achieving excellence and professional stability in the technology field.

FINAL CONCLUSION

Throughout this book, we have explored the many facets of C#, covering everything from its fundamentals to advanced applications in areas like artificial intelligence, IoT, and game development. This chapter revisits the most important lessons from each section, reflecting on C#'s impact on the modern world and emphasizing the importance of investing in continuous learning.

Summary of the Main Lessons

Chapter 1. Introduction to C#: History and Applications

We introduced the evolution of C# from its creation to becoming one of the most widely used languages globally. We explored its practical applications, highlighting how it is fundamental in areas such as web development, gaming, and enterprise systems.

Chapter 2. Setting Up Your Development Environment

We demonstrated how to set up the development environment with Visual Studio and alternatives, as well as running simple programs. "Hello, World!" was used as the basis to introduce interaction with debugging tools.

Chapter 3. Structure of a C# Program

We analyzed the structure of C# programs, addressing elements such as namespaces, classes, and methods. We also discussed coding conventions and naming patterns to improve code readability and maintainability.

Chapter 4. Data Types and Operators

We studied primitive and composite data types and explored arithmetic, relational, and logical operators. These tools are essential for creating efficient solutions in any application.

Chapter 5. Flow Control in C#

Conditional structures (if, else, switch) and loops (for, while, foreach) were detailed, showing how to control the program's flow of execution.

Chapter 6. Functions and Methods

This chapter covered creating and using functions, exploring variable scope, parameter passing, static and instance methods.

Chapter 7. Classes, Objects, and OOP

We covered object-oriented programming, highlighting concepts such as encapsulation, inheritance, and polymorphism. Properties and interfaces were introduced as key tools for building modular and reusable systems.

Chapter 8. String Manipulation

We learned to work with strings, performing operations like formatting, searching, and replacement. Regular expressions were presented as a powerful way to handle textual data.

Chapter 9. Collections and Data Structures

We explored collections such as arrays, lists, and dictionaries, as well as discussing common operations and best practices for handling large volumes of data.

Chapter 10. Exception Handling

We discussed the importance of handling errors safely and efficiently using try, catch, and finally. Custom exceptions were created to improve error message clarity.

Chapter 11. Working with Files

We covered reading and writing files, manipulating streams, and data serialization. These skills are fundamental for applications that deal with local storage or data exchange between systems.

Chapter 12. Asynchronous Programming with C#

We learned about async/await, task management, and multithreading. Asynchronous programming was presented as an indispensable tool for scalable and high-performance systems.

Chapter 13. LINQ: Language Integrated Query

We studied LINQ as a powerful solution for manipulating

collections and accessing databases declaratively, simplifying complex tasks.

Chapter 14. Development with Windows Forms

We introduced the creation of basic graphical interfaces, event handling, and connecting UI elements to business logic.

Chapter 15. Web Development with ASP.NET

This chapter explored ASP.NET Core for building web applications and RESTful APIs. We discussed the fundamentals of MVC and implementing scalable services.

Chapter 16. Database Integration

We learned to connect applications to databases like SQL Server, performing CRUD operations and using frameworks such as Entity Framework to simplify data access.

Chapter 17. Game Applications with Unity

We discovered how to develop games with Unity, using C# to implement interactions, animations, and game logic.

Chapter 18. Security and Best Practices

We discussed the importance of input validation, vulnerability prevention, and recommended practices for creating secure applications.

Chapter 19. Testing and Debugging Code

This chapter addressed debugging techniques in Visual Studio and the creation of unit tests with NUnit, as well as the use of test automation tools.

Chapter 20. Optimization and Performance

We presented strategies to improve code efficiency, reduce memory usage, and measure performance with tools like BenchmarkDotNet.

Chapter 21. Working with External APIs

We studied how to consume REST and SOAP APIs, authenticate with OAuth, and work with real-time services using WebSockets.

Chapter 22. C# for IoT and Devices

We explored programming IoT devices, communication with sensors and actuators, and practical automation using C#.

Chapter 23. Real-World Projects with C#

We presented practical projects, such as a task management system and a secure API, to apply the concepts learned.

Chapter 24. Future Trends in C#

We discussed .NET innovations and the impact of C# in emerging areas such as AI, IoT, and cloud computing.

Chapter 25. Career Tips and Certifications

We concluded with guidance for career planning, relevant certifications, and technical interview preparation, highlighting how continuous learning is essential for success.

Reflection on the Importance of C#

C# is more than just a programming language: it's a passport to the future of technology. Its versatility allows for the development of robust, scalable, and innovative systems, whether creating enterprise solutions, interactive games, or connected devices. Investing in learning C# means being prepared to lead digital transformation and build a lasting impact in a competitive market.

We sincerely thank you for dedicating your time and effort to learning this material. Your choice to invest in C# reflects a commitment to excellence and a genuine desire to progress in your career. We are honored to be part of your journey and hope this book serves as a reliable guide in your professional evolution.

Sincerely,
Diego Rodrigues and Team!